C000230577

Psychology of MOTORSPORT SUCCESS

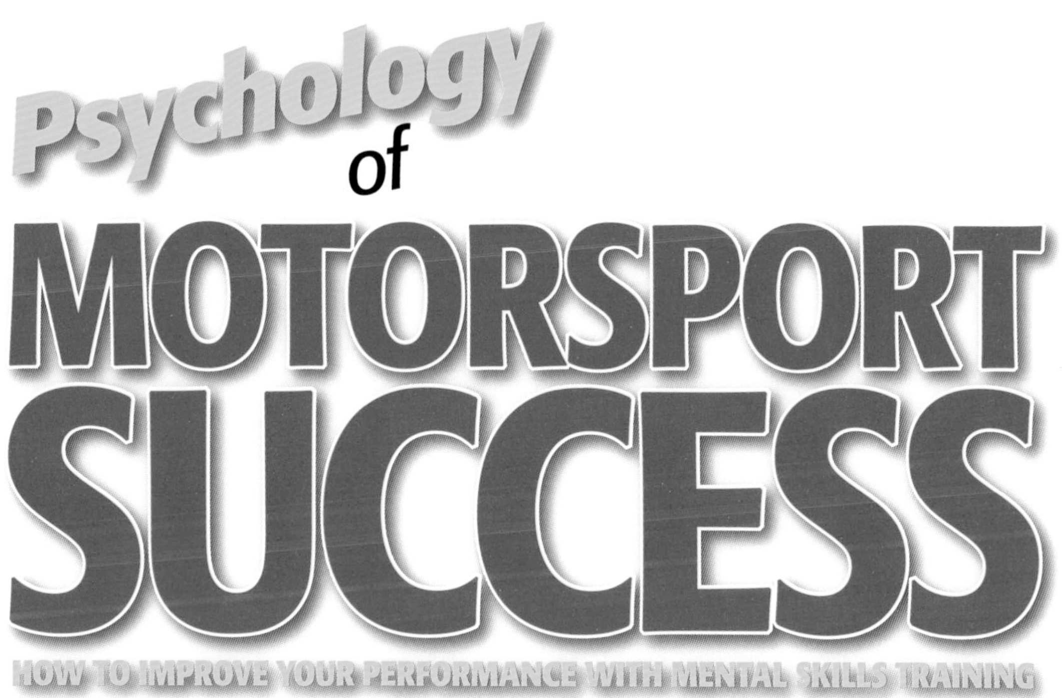

Dr Paul Castle

Foreword by John Surtees MBE

Haynes Publishing

First published in April 2008

A catalogue record for this book is available from the British Library

ISBN 978 1 84425 495 8

Library of Congress catalog card no. 2007943095

Published by Haynes Publishing, Sparkford, Yeovil, Somerset BA22 7JJ, UK

Tel: 01963 442030 Fax: 01963 440001
Int. tel: +44 1963 442030 Int. fax: +44 1963 440001
E-mail: sales@haynes.co.uk
Website: www.haynes.co.uk

Haynes North America, Inc.,
861 Lawrence Drive, Newbury Park,
California 91320, USA

Printed and bound in England by
J. H. Haynes & Co. Ltd, Sparkford

Contents

Acknowledgements

I WOULD LIKE TO ACKNOWLEDGE the support of the following people, without whom this book would not have reached fruition. First and foremost, thanks must go to Mark Hughes at Haynes Publishing, for putting up with my persistence; and also to Steve Rendle at Haynes, for easing the burden on my shoulders at different stages of the writing process. Secondly, I would like to thank Brain-Tuned Sport Psychology Solutions, who provided the backdrop against which I was able to develop and hone my craft; and Paul Rees, General Manager of Centurion Racing, whose support at a crucial stage in the writing of this book was invaluable.

I would also like to acknowledge the donation of images by Aston Martin Racing, Caterham Cars, Centurion Racing, Ross Curnow, Nick Plumb at Touratech UK, Rimstock plc, Volkswagen UK and Kevin F. York. Thanks are also due to Dave Willoughby at David.WillowPhotography.co.uk for allowing me to raid his catalogue, and to Nick Boot-Handford for 'operationalising' the schematic illustrations. I hope my writing does justice to their professionalism.

I also need to thank my colleagues Clare Rhoden and Julia West in the School of Sport and Exercise Science, University of Worcester, for their support and often surreal yet stimulating input that challenged my mind as I wrote. Further thanks are owed to Clare for her comments on a pre-submission draft. Thanks must also go to Annie Lambeth for her contribution to Chapter 6. Your expertise has made an important contribution to this book. Also, I must acknowledge Drs Jan Graydon, Iain Greenlees, Tim Holder and Terry McMorris for acting as academic catalysts for much of the information contained herein.

I would like to thank the numerous racers who have helped to provide the material for this text – confidentiality prevents me from naming you! Their race-craft prompted many changes to the guidance offered, which otherwise simply wouldn't have worked in the way that it does in 'slower' sports. Also, Gary Stubbington, Alan Hesleden and Chris Moore. It has been a pleasure, guys. I'm unsure which one of us has the tightest psychological straitjacket, but at least we can discuss the fastest way of getting the buckles undone. Crazy folk! Also, to Clive, Pam and Lucy Jones. It is good to see you getting 'back on track.' Keep going!

My thanks go to Gaye Arnold for her literary skills, kind words and comments on evolving drafts of the manuscript. Your passion for the English language is addictive. I'm hooked! Also to Prof Steve van Toller for setting me on the right track. Thank you.

I would like to thank Nita for her continuing support over the years, Kianna for her smile, enquiring mind and humour … and finally Nikki, for just being. You are so important to me. Kind, loving, witty, 'extreme', and always there when I am in danger of missing the apex. The way in which you have overcome your own challenges are testament to your abilities. Stay focused!

I would like to take this opportunity to thank John Surtees for taking time out of his busy schedule to comment on this book. It is a privilege to receive feedback from such an emminent figure in motorsport.

The completion of this book corresponds with the achievements of one person who epitomises everything I believe and everything I have attempted to disseminate in the forthcoming pages. There has never been a better advertisement for motor sport psychology than now. Congratulations to Lewis Hamilton, whose achievements in his inaugural F1 season are truly outstanding!

Dr Paul Castle
April 2008

Foreword

by John Surtees MBE

PSYCHOLOGY OF COURSE is a part of our everyday life, but the world and environment in which we live is ever changing and the challenges that this represents causes us all to take a closer look at ourselves in how we meet those challenges.

In the world of sport we are forever seeing examples of talent being squandered by the sports person not being able to focus on how best to use their ability. In motorsport I think it is possibly fair to say that it has only been since the advent of worldwide television and the sponsorship revenue that is generated for the teams that they have looked at the larger picture in more detail in order to get a competitive edge. Driver programmes associated with physical and mental fitness have had a high priority, with of course sport psychology playing its part.

John Surtees won the 500cc World Championship four times for MV Augusta, in 1956, 1958, 1959 and 1960. (Nick Nicholls)

Previously a driver or rider just had to perform and sort his own problems out; a possible exception being in the lead up to World War II and the tremendous effort that Mercedes-Benz and Auto Union made in Grand Prix car racing. But then, until relatively recent years, the pattern of the competitor was different. They were generally in their twenties with a greater amount of experience and maturity.

The sports person of today is quite different and, if we concentrate on motorsport, we are talking about competition starting at 8 years of age. If you take Lewis Hamilton, at 23 years of age we have a young man who has been racing for 15 years. He has had to contend with not just growing up and all that means, but with education and the pressures that a competitive scene, like a race circuit, particularly if you are successful, can bring.

I know there have been times in my life when I needed help. I think generally I have spent a large part of my life during an age when there were less pressures than one is currently confronted with. In my involvement with young drivers, including my son, I have seen first-hand the demons with which they are at times confronted. It is all happening so early in life for many of these competitors and, just for a moment, they need to be at times helped to find themselves and to be able to truly focus on making the very best use of their ability. I suppose you could say there needs to be a little team work and sport psychology has to be a major part of that team.

John Surtees
February 2008

John Surtees remains the only man to have won World Championships on two and four wheels, and is seen here driving a Ferrari 158 in the British Grand Prix at Brands Hatch during his 1964 Formula 1 World Championship-winning season. (Phipps/Sutton)

Preface

PSYCHOLOGY IMPACTS on every minute of every day of our lives. The decisions we make are founded upon our thoughts, beliefs, principles and morals. Our decisions are coloured by emotional states and/or stressful experiences. If we feel aggressive, we are more likely to compete aggressively, and this, in turn, is likely to be detrimental to performance. We succumb to fatigue and loss of concentration at the most inopportune of moments and we lack self-confidence as a result of a 'poor run of form'. There are days when we lack passion, drive and motivation; and other days on which we are ready to take on the world.

Regardless of these potentially damaging elements washing around in your mind, you expect to take the controls of your racing bike or car, fire up the engine, and exit the pit garage completely focused and ready to 'go to work'. Yes, there will be days when nothing will break through the mental armour. There will be days when you can't put a foot wrong and when you are seemingly invincible. Yet everyone else on the circuit may feel exactly the same way. *Then* you have a race on your hands, and it is the competitor with the strongest mental resolve and the will to win who will come through the battle unscathed.

Motorsport psychology is an area of sport psychology that focuses on 'identifying and understanding psychological theories and interventions [solutions] that can be applied to sport and exercise to enhance the performance and personal growth of athletes and physical activity participants' (Williams and Straub, 2006, p.1). Whether you like it or not, you cannot escape from psychology. It informs (or misinforms) what you think and how you act or react to situations in which you find yourself.

The key to successful racing is not having one of those 'do no wrong' days. The key to successful racing is consistency, and the following chapters will do two things. Firstly, they will help you to acknowledge the elements that need to be considered in striving to become, or remain, successful in racing. Secondly, they will guide you through the techniques that will help in developing the skills necessary to become psychologically strong when it matters.

Chapter 1

Introduction

Motorsport rewards winners

Much of racing is based wholeheartedly on a system of rewards and punishments. If you perform well, you will keep your ride or drive; if you perform poorly, you will lose it. Reward and punishment. If you win, you will receive a trophy; if you

Perform well and the rewards are high. (LAT)

come fourth, you will receive some points; but if you come 16th or lower in the field, you will receive nothing! Similarly, if you are performing well you may, perhaps, receive preferential treatment from other sources, such as suppliers; but if you do poorly, you may lose your helmet sponsor or another contributory sponsorship. Thinking in this way is detrimental to your racing, yet I encounter it almost everywhere I go. 'I must do well,' 'I must win,' 'I really have to do well,' are familiar comments. But it is *not* the doing well or winning that is important. It is the focusing on *what* you are doing that is important, that is within your control, and will be far more likely to lead to a successful result. You need to imprint this message deep in your brain from this chapter onwards. I will make this point time and time again.

How can motorsport psychology help you become a winner?

My preferred method of providing support is to adopt a cognitive-behavioural approach. This means that, throughout this book, I aim to guide you in examining and changing the way in which you think about your racing (the cognitive component). Sometimes, however, a 'quick fix' is required. Under these circumstances I tend to use what I call the 'elastoplast technique', examining the way in which you might act in such situations (the behavioural component). Behaviour that is cause for concern may then be modified or adapted appropriately so that performance improves in those situations.

I call this the 'elastoplast technique' because it does little more than solve the problem temporarily. It is not a definitive solution. The best analogy I can give is the humble headache tablet. You may take a headache tablet when you have a headache, because it is the 'quick fix'. What you should really do is establish what caused the headache in the first place, so that you can prevent it from happening in future. Similarly, if you have no confidence in pushing the front end as you enter turn 4, I would perhaps suggest easing off the throttle a little more than usual for the remainder of the session and then trying to discover the source of the issue before the second session.

Psychological weakness or psychological skills training (PST)?

The idea that psychological weakness is a bad thing is unhelpful. In the same way, negative connotations associated with the words 'psychological' or 'mental' are unhelpful. If you lack knowledge or practical experience in any of the themes contained in this book, it might simply mean that you have never thought it important, or even that you were never aware that it would help your racing. Simply acknowledging the importance of psychology in motorsport is not enough. It is crucial that the psychological skills techniques that you will acquire through reading this book are practised until they become second nature. If I had £1 for

OPPOSITE: *Free your mind of weaknesses and focus on the challenge facing you.* (LAT)

JOHNNIE WALKER
Mobil
1

every time people have asked if I work with competitors who have 'psychological problems', I would be rich. This is not what a sport psychologist does. It is important that you understand the flavour of this book: I expect you to build on your present 'psychological starting point'.

Psychological skills training will help you build on your present mental foundations

PST is a systematic, educational programme designed to help you acquire and practise performance-enhancing psychological skills. It offers a positive approach, focusing on the acquisition of new skills in areas of 'weakness' (I prefer using the word, 'challenge'), rather than focusing on what racers should not be doing. As soon as you recognise that psychological skills can be used to improve your performance, you are already well on the road to success. As you progress through this book you will learn how to develop these skills and practise them, and you will then be ready to incorporate them into your 'racing brain'.

However, I have a word of warning regarding reasonable expectations. PST takes a little time and effort. Do not expect results in one week! You would not expect to become a professional racer after one week in a car or on a racing bike, so why should acquiring PST techniques be any different? Think of it as an investment of valuable time in acquiring the necessary skills to improve performance, reduce your lap times and push harder. You should avoid the 'quick fix' wherever possible, because it has a tendency to bite you on the backside at the most inopportune moments.

By using PST successfully you will avoid over-training physically and under-training psychologically. The aim is for you to be at the peak of optimal physical and psychological performance at the same time ... as the lights go out and you exit the grid.

Openness and honesty

It is imperative, in reading this book, that you are open and honest with yourself in your thoughts about your ability and performances. What I really mean here is that competitors might not always present the full picture of their situation. Sport psychologists are trained to explore various avenues in order to gain sufficient information to help resolve any emerging issues. Obviously, this is not possible in a book. However, in order to gain maximum benefit you should feel comfortable enough to think about the type of information you might need to get out into the open in order to make progress. Of course, it might be the case that you are unaware of the source of the difficulties. This is fine and perfectly understandable. This book will help to draw out some of the possible difficulties you are experiencing.

You will get the most from this book if you evaluate yourself at the personal level. This is the level at which you would not share your thoughts with anyone else at all. This is the level of complete honesty. It is the level at which you might not divulge detail to the media, or even to your own team, but is the 'real' reason for your performance. If a lack of performance is a consequence of a 'failing' within yourself, this book provides possible solutions as the facts present themselves. Needless to say, under normal consultancy terms it takes time to establish a working rapport with people in order for this level of openness to be attained. Nevertheless, a sport psychologist should endeavour to ensure that their service is sufficient to foster a safe context in which both parties can work effectively together.

There will be occasions when you do not wish to acknowledge or accept the case that you may be at fault. Let's face it: human nature is such that no one likes being wrong. The successful competitor will be the one who accepts and evaluates faults, develops ways around these faults and moves on, having learnt from them. 'Fault' is nothing more than a label for something that needs to be changed in order for an improvement to be made. If competitors accept this, there is no longer any need for negative feelings, which, incidentally, do nothing more than cause further psychological damage.

Ethical principles and confidentiality

Complementing openness and honesty, the protection given by sports psychologists' membership of professional bodies ensures that a code of conduct is followed at all times. Sports psychologists are bound by principles of ethics and confidentiality. Indeed, you will not see me name a particular person with a specific 'problem' in this book. This would be unethical. Codes of ethics can be found on all of the websites listed later in this chapter. In short, the sport psychologist will not do anything to cause psychological harm, trauma or suffering to clients.

A key principle in working with clients is the maintenance of confidentiality at all times. You should appreciate that, in order to offer suitable support, a sport psychologist will need to acquire personal and sometimes sensitive information. It goes without saying that such information should not be made public. There are occasions when people around a competitor might need to be made aware of any issues that arise as a result of meetings with the sport psychologist, if performance is to change. However, such information should not be divulged without the consent of the client. The sport psychologist should ensure that the right information is disseminated to the right people at the right time and with full agreement from the client. A sport psychologist may overcome this potential area of difficulty by preparing the client to communicate their needs directly with the people concerned.

A comment about 'context'

It is important at this early stage to consider the importance of context in the great scheme of things. Sport psychologists should be aware of the dynamics behind racing (the bigger picture) and need to be mindful that providing guidance to a competitor might only be part of the story. There may be occasions when the sport psychologist might be thinking about the effects of too much caffeine, or insufficient hydration, which may be causing difficulties in concentration. Indeed, a racer with a head cold once told me that he was unable to focus fully on his position entering corners. Consequently he was unable to enter corners in the normal way because he felt 'weird'. I advised him that it was possibly because the virus was affecting his balance and spatial orientation, and was not a reflection on his apparent, sudden inability to ride a racing bike.

On other occasions the sport psychologist might be thinking about how the racer is interacting with team personnel and whether he or she is displaying signs of anxiety or stress. Alternatively, the sport psychologist may be interested in exploring how the team, corporate sponsors and/or the general public are behaving around the racer. I have managed to solve problems by diplomatically asking people around the racer to adapt their own behaviour. This has had sudden, positive effects on the racer's psychological state and, ultimately, on performance.

Access to specialists in motorsport psychology

There are relatively few sport psychologists in the UK who specialise in motorsport. Those of us who do are more than likely accredited by the British Psychological Society (BPS) or the British Association for Sport and Exercise Sciences (BASES). Both of these bodies are internationally recognised, as are their counterparts in other countries. In the USA, for example, the equivalent body to BASES is AAASP, the Association for the Advancement of Applied Sport Psychology, while the American Psychological Association is the equivalent body to the BPS. All of these professional bodies have an internet presence, and their sites are a goldmine of information about the profession. Further information can be found at the following URLs:

- www.bps.org.uk
- www.bases.org.uk
- www.aaasponline.org

It is recommended that anyone seeking support is aware that these bodies exist for the protection of both the 'consumer' and the practitioner. Certain criteria must be met in order to gain accreditation and standards must be maintained in order to retain it. So, accreditation, or chartered status, means that a sport psychologist is sufficiently qualified to provide high quality support, in the same way that holding a racing licence means you are sufficiently competent to race. Sport psychologists will invariably be keen to keep abreast of modern developments in their discipline, by scanning relevant academic journals, attending workshops or conferences and passing this knowledge on to you, the consumer.

Summary

In this introductory chapter I have set the scene by providing an idea of how the way in which you think can influence your performance in competition. I have also shown how the role of sport psychology is often overlooked in motorsport and is something that might make the difference between first place and yet another DNF.

I have also, I hope, laid your mind at rest in pointing out that sport psychology support is governed by ethical principles and guidelines, laid down by the relevant professional bodies both nationally and internationally. Consequently, if you seek guidance from a sport psychologist you can be assured of receiving a high standard of consultancy. Sport psychologists do not take their discipline lightly and constantly strive to update their knowledge through continuing professional development. Indeed, at our Sport Performance & Coaching Centre at the University of Worcester we strive to deliver nothing less than a high-quality service informed by current thinking.

I reiterate the point that sport psychologists are non-judgemental and do not attribute blame to their clients for 'failings'. Rather, we use any information collected to help improve aspects of a competitor's psychological profile to enhance performance. These days it seems that people live in a 'blame' culture. Yet blame is not productive or helpful. It is destructive and puts barriers in the way of progress. It does not change what has happened, and will not change the result, since you are unable to go back and do things differently. The only option is to look to the future, to what happens next and to how you might improve for the next race. Once a competitor understands this, the way forward will become so much clearer.

Metaphorically speaking, you are now standing on the top board, ready to dive into the complex world of motorsport psychology. The following chapters appear in no particular order of importance and you should not see them as building on top of each other. Rather, I would like you to take each one as an ingredient in a recipe. It doesn't matter which ingredient you put into the mix first, only that you put *all* of the ingredients in. You can decide how little or how much after you have read each chapter and decided on its relevance to your own situation.

Chapter 2

Attention and concentration

PICTURE THE SCENE. The starting grid is full. Pit crew and 'brolly dollies' are milling around the motor cycles. The crowd looks on in anticipation. Grid personnel are discussing tactics with you and making small talk. You take a drink to maintain hydration levels and wait for the one-minute signal. The signal sounds, the grid empties of personnel and you are left to focus on the start. You leave the grid on the warm-up lap, get some heat into the tyres and settle into your task. As the competitors take their places on the grid for the start you pull up into position and wait. Engines rev ... the lights go out and ... you make a terrible start. Why is this? You know how to make a good start from standstill. You have done so, many times. Yet now, when it really matters, your attention is focused elsewhere. It is not quick enough. It somehow does not communicate with your throttle and clutch hands to produce the start that you desperately desire.

Similarly, during the race you are suddenly block-passed by an opponent. This throws your concentration and you start to drop off the pace. It takes you a while to regain focus, but by this time it is too late to catch the lead pack again. If only you could switch your focus on again, but quicker.

These two examples suggest that focusing attention is essential in the successful performance of sporting tasks. Lack of concentration or the focusing of attention on inappropriate things may be extremely detrimental and may ultimately affect the outcome of a race. This chapter addresses some of the reasons why this might happen and discusses ways in which attentional focus may be improved.

Clarifying terminology

Attention and concentration are not the same, although the two terms are used interchangeably. As a result, defining concentration is not as easy as you might

OPPOSITE: *Regaining your focus after a distraction is an important skill to learn.* (David.WillowPhotography.co.uk)

SHOEI
AVVIO
blackhorse
SPYKE
SHOEI
Vent-Axia
VK
sbs
Vent-Axia
Stobart
SPYKE
DUCATI

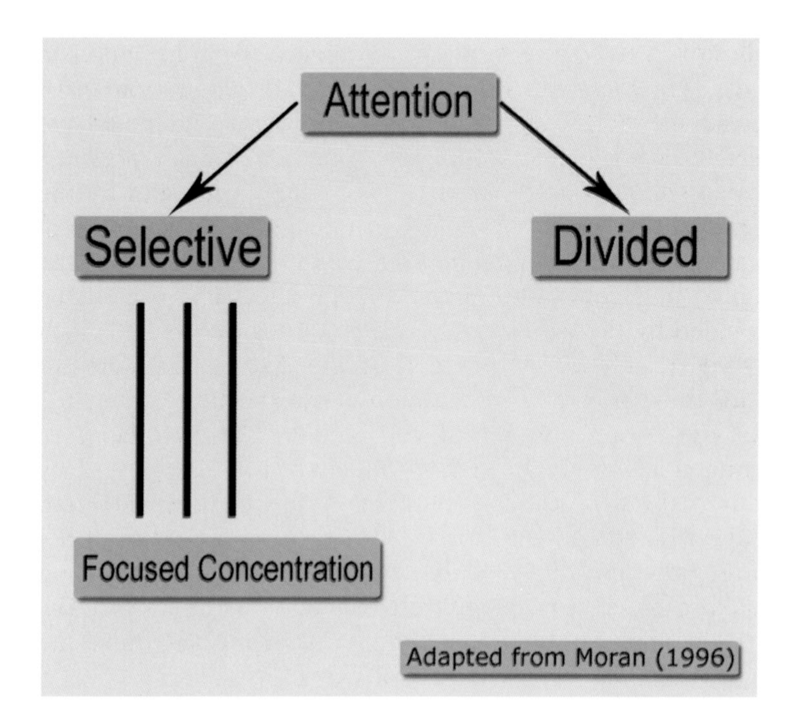

A racer's attention may initially take one of two directions. (Boot-Handford/Author)

hope. In this section I highlight the differences between attention, attentional focus and concentration, so that you are clear about the link between them.

The schematic diagram above shows how attention can be subdivided. I will use the term 'attentional focus' when referring to concentration. You may use either term. However, in my opinion, the term 'attentional focus' provides a form of key phrase, similar to those discussed in Chapter 10 on self-talk. It tells you to 'focus your attention'. The question in your mind should be 'on what?', and you then actively search the environment for relevant cues. To say 'concentrate' is perhaps rather too vague and woolly. It is akin to saying 'relax' when you might not know how to.

Attention

Attention was originally defined, by the psychologist William James over a hundred years ago, as processing 'one out of what seem several simultaneously possible objects or trains of thought … It implies withdrawal from some things in order to deal effectively with others' (James, 1890, pp.403–4). This means that you selectively attend to a single mental thought, and it is this thought that goes forward in the mind.

However, attention is far more than this. Despite age-old, humorous comments about the alleged differences between male and female brains, the capacity of the human brain to process several pieces of information simultaneously is evident. It is also widely accepted that attention is selective, but in a more complicated way, *ie* the individual is able actively to attend to relevant stimuli in the environment. Consider the times when you have overheard someone else mention your name in conversation and you have 'tuned in', as it were, to this conversation. Of course, in motorsport the importance of selective attention is no different. As you wait on the grid for the lights to go out, you must filter out irrelevant information such as the sound of the crowd or the commentator over the tannoy. You need to attend selectively to the sound of the engine, the feel of the clutch and throttle balance, and the visual information provided by the lights. As the lights go out, you must launch the machine smoothly yet quickly off the line and begin selectively attending to the visual cues that are now providing information about the first corner, the position of opponents, the desired line etc. If you consider the importance of selective attention during ordinary daily activities, you have to be impressed by the way in which your brain is processing information and focusing attention when speeds are in excess of 100mph and allow little time for error. Most, if not all, of your senses are providing information and your brain assembles and processes it before making a decision on the best course of action as you exit turn 2. Before you know it, your brain is going through exactly the same procedure for turns 3, 4 and 5, all within a matter of a few seconds.

Attentional focus

Attentional focus is the term psychologists use to describe the ability to attend to relevant information during competitive events. Environmental cues may be relevant or irrelevant to task performance. A concept called 'attentional narrowing' refers to the broadening or narrowing of this focus. In other words, attentional narrowing reduces available cues within the environment, so that cues are used or utilised effectively. This is like the zoom function on your digital camera. One is the broad/narrow perspective, in which we take a wide or narrow view and process many, or few, aspects of the environment; the other is the internal/external perspective, in which we view the environment either from within or outside of ourselves. I will discuss this in more detail shortly.

Concentration

Concentration is a prerequisite for success. It is about being totally immersed in the here and now. The past and future are not important. Your focus on the present seems effortless and you could race all day if necessary.

Psychologists suggest that competitors should use one of two strategies to help maintain concentration:

Learn to increase attention to relevant information – this involves training yourself to focus on anything that will help you to do the job, *eg* the sensitivity of accelerator/throttle control.

Learn to decrease attention to irrelevant stimuli – this involves training yourself to shut out anything that may hinder your concentration, *eg* the flag waving at turn 5, whose message favours your opponent.

After you have become practised in each strategy, I would favour learning how to use a combination of both. Filtering relevant information into conscious awareness is usually a good thing, since it is a positive attempt to increase awareness. Blocking irrelevant information from entering your mind is more risky, because at some point in your racing the very thing you are blocking will creep in, and if this happens during the biggest race of your career you will not be too pleased! I would rather let something irrelevant enter my mind so that I can actively evaluate and dismiss it. Think of it in terms of a Teflon coating on a frying pan. You can throw anything into the pan but nothing will stick – it simply washes off.

Some sport psychologists propose that concentration comprises four elements:

- Focusing selectively is necessary.
- Focus should be maintained over an undisclosed period of time.
- You should be aware of the unfolding situation.
- You should be able to alter attentional focus as required.

In *Sport Psychology: Contemporary Themes* (2004), David Lavallee and his colleagues include an additional element for successful concentration that they call 'time-sharing'. This is simply another name for dividing your attention. In motorsport terms, I have no doubt that you are able to divide your attention between overtaking a slower opponent on the brakes into Druids at Brands Hatch while simultaneously paying attention to taking your preferred racing line.

Components of attention

Many theories of attention exist but to outline all of them would be a book in its own right. It is, however, possible to summarise them into three main categories, all of which have some relevance to motorsport. Attention can be viewed as a filter; a spotlight; or a resource.

Attention as a filter

One way to think of attention is as a filter or funnel through which many pieces of information enter the brain, but only one of these pieces is actually processed. If you believe that you can only concentrate on one thing at a time, this way of thinking is relevant for you. If you do think in this way, I would challenge you and would aim to work towards showing you that you can process more than a single piece of information at any given moment.

Attention as a spotlight

Attentional focus can also be regarded as being like the beam of a spotlight, used to pick up relevant information in a similar way to a police helicopter searching for suspects at night. You are flexible in where you 'direct the beam'. If you are able to direct your thoughts towards specific things on track, this suggests that you are already able to focus attention. This does not mean to say that you cannot improve on using this strategy. However, it does help to identify relevant stimuli on which to focus. It also provides an explanation for what happens when you lose concentration: focusing on the right area for too long or focusing on the wrong area.

Attention as a resource

Another way of thinking about attentional focus is as being like a 'pool' with a limited capacity. The analogy I use with my students is of a beer glass. As the beer is poured into the glass, there is a point at which the glass will not hold any more than its capacity. If you keep pouring, the beer will simply overflow and be wasted. In the same way, information entering your mind will fill the available space until you can no longer concentrate on new input. Some sport psychologists believe that there is not one 'pool' but many, so, in practical racing terms, you may have a 'vehicle-control' resource-pool, a 'strategy' resource-pool, an 'engine-evaluation' resource-pool and so on. These are not necessarily the same size, so you may be able to focus more easily on one pool because it is 'larger' than another. Of course, you might direct the spotlight beam, discussed above, onto one of these pools. A nice idea! The sport psychologist and competitor should work together to identify the types of resource-pool needed for the task, and work towards switching attentional focus between each of these at appropriate moments in time, without negatively affecting performance.

Different types of attentional focus

As I mentioned above, your attention seems to be drawn to both relevant and irrelevant cues in the environment. Even as you read this chapter, you are being distracted by the noise outside, the dog, the children playing or the ticking of the clock ... at least, you are now that I have drawn your attention to them! Sport psychologists generally agree that physiological arousal levels influence whether a competitor will filter relevant or irrelevant cues for processing in the brain. The schematic diagram below illustrates this nicely. Attentional input can be seen as a funnel lying on its side. Initially, all sensory information enters the funnel. Some of it is relevant (represented by a plus sign) and some irrelevant (represented by a zero). The horizontal axis represents level of arousal and the two vertical red lines represent the area of processing where relevant information is filtered in while irrelevant information is filtered out. You should notice that this happens at a moderate level of arousal. This is the essence of Easterbrook's theory: a moderate

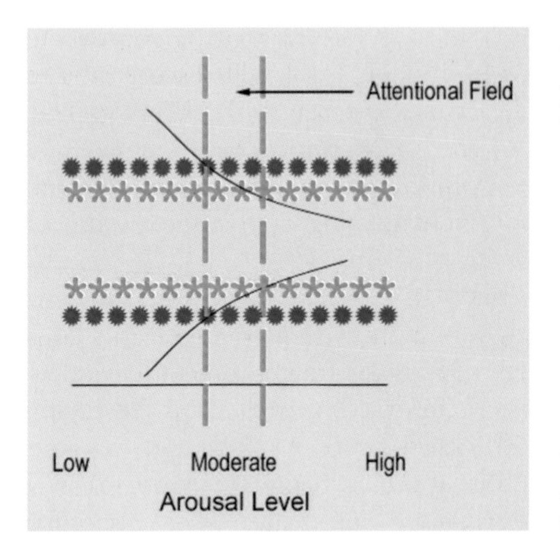

Moderate levels of arousal should improve your attentional focus. (Boot-Handford/Author)

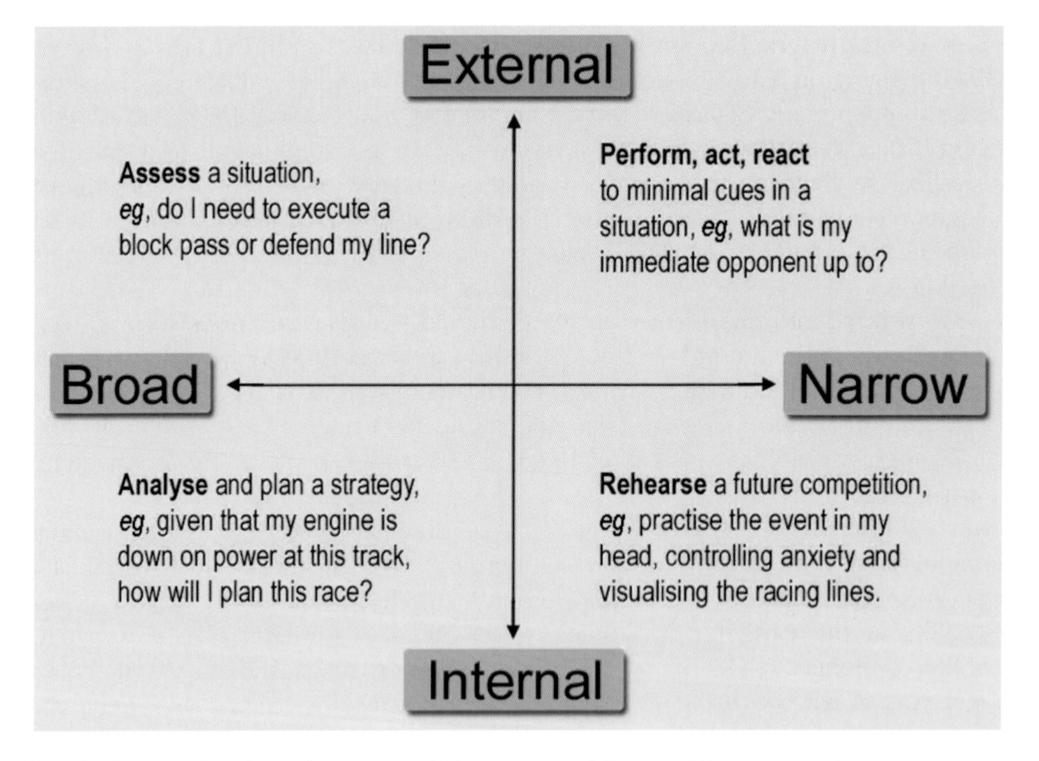

Attentional focus may shift depending on your needs at a specific moment in time. (Boot-Handford/Author)

level of arousal is best for successful attentional focus. Of course, it is not quite as straightforward as that. The sport psychologist would need to establish what 'moderate' means for individual competitors, and this would undoubtedly differ from person to person.

Robert Nideffer maintains that attention can be viewed along the dimensions of direction and width. By 'direction' he means whether information is internal or external. For example, a marathon runner may adopt an internal perspective to focus on information about how his or her body feels. As I will discuss later, a racer may focus on internal cues, such as heart rate just before the lights go out, as a way of checking whether arousal levels are too high or not. Alternatively, a racer may focus on external cues such as something in the environment, like an oil patch on the start-finish straight, an opponent coming up on the inside, or debris on the track.

By 'width', Nideffer means whether one adopts a broad or a narrow perspective. A broad perspective enables the competitor to process various cues simultaneously. If you are racing down the start-finish straight amidst a pack of three or four opponents, you will be aware of information regarding the racing line for the next corner, dips, ripples etc, as well as the position of your opponents, their lines and so on. This information may allow you to make a rapid decision about what to do on the approach. This is attentional focus for the present. In contrast, a narrow perspective allows the competitor to hone in on or one or maybe two specific things. In torrential rain during the 2005 Moto GP at Donington Park, Valentino Rossi seemed to sit behind Marco Mellandri without making any rash moves for lap after lap. I would anticipate that he was using a narrow attentional focus to assess Mellandri's weaknesses and his own strengths so that he could plan a strategy for the most effective and least dangerous overtake. Interestingly, I would also anticipate that Rossi was adopting a broad attentional focus to oversee how the race overall was unfolding.

You will fall into one of the four quadrants in the diagram opposite. However, you will also move around these quadrants at different times, because your brain will be processing different information as time passes. Of course, the hard part is to actually move around these quadrants at the right time. This is where the role of the sport psychologist is invaluable, and the next few pages will give you some guidance regarding what to focus on.

I will provide a classic example of a situation that I am certain many competitors will identify with, in which you are focusing only on your immediate opponent (*ie* employing a narrow, external focus). Your only concern is to overtake at the earliest opportunity, when, all of a sudden, out of nowhere another opponent overtakes both of you and storms off into the distance. Your focus was so narrow that you were unable to perceive the wider picture. Mastery of attentional focus will be the key that unlocks your concentration during performances. It will not prevent things from happening out on the track, but, with practice, it won't phase you and you will be able to redirect your attention to the new demands of the situation.

Regardless of which quadrant you are in at any given moment, the message of this section is very clear: attentional focus may be adversely influenced by many potential distractions, both in the environment and within yourself.

Attentional distractors

As I am sure you are aware from personal experience, there are many distractions during race weekends that can take your mind away from the task in hand, or divert your attention to inappropriate aspects of the environment. At a general level, these can be divided nicely into internal and external distractors. One of the first things you should do, when addressing concentration problems, is to identify whether distractors are internal or external.

Internal distractors

As one might expect, these are internalised concerns and worries about a competition. They are thoughts and cognitions that are of little, if any, benefit to performance, and include: reflecting on past events; predicting future events; choking under pressure; fatigue; and motivation.

Reflecting on past events

Reflecting on the past is not necessarily a good thing in motorsport. It is akin to superstition. 'I always do well at Silverstone.' 'I always crash at Cadwell Park.' 'I nearly came off every time I came out of turn 3.' Mentally, this sets the mind up to do the same thing again next time. It is a way of convincing yourself that the past will influence the present. Of course, having experience and knowledge are good qualities in racing. However, they can work against you unless you use them wisely to inform your performance. In response to the quotations above, I usually suggest that the competitor works in 'the here and now'. I agree that reflection on past experiences is a good thing in helping to identify weaknesses and highlight successful performances. However, it is not beneficial when a new competitive race weekend is in progress.

Predicting future events

Fortune-telling, or predicting what will happen at the current race weekend, is another self-induced distraction that can have adverse effects on competitors. Such distractions are relatively easy to spot, since they usually consist of 'what if?' statements. For example, 'What if I get a poor start?' 'What if I crash?' Or even, 'What if I don't do well for the team?' By avoiding such statements and focusing instead on the present, on strategy and on your own performance- or process-related goals, you will not succumb to these distractions.

Another type of future-based distraction is where a thought seems to suddenly drop into your head, such as, 'How am I going to get to the airport next Wednesday?' Of course, this has nothing to do with the present race weekend, but nevertheless, it is an unwanted and unhelpful distraction. In the chapter on self-talk, I mention using key words to regain focus. In preparing you for dealing with unwanted thoughts, I would perhaps advise you to use the word, 'STOP' as an immediate flag to show that the 'airport' thought is a distractor. I would then help you to substitute the distractor thought with a more appropriate replacement thought, such as, 'I will hit the apex just beyond that ripple in the track.' Of course, you must practise this technique before being able to use it successfully. The sport psychologist's role in this instance would be to help you to identify when thoughts of this type may emerge and to deal with them accordingly. The distracting thought could be anything from getting to the airport to a wedding anniversary, but the content is unimportant. The key is having the correct tool to solve the problem.

Choking under pressure

I am sure that at some point in your motorsport career you have succumbed to pressure – perhaps because you have moved up to a higher level of competition; perhaps because you have received a major sponsorship deal and are expected to perform; or perhaps because there are 20,000 spectators and the event is being televised. Such factors may lead to 'choking' under pressure. Your performance suddenly drops through the floor. When it finally came to the crunch, you were unable to perform. Some people would argue that this is a bad thing and, yes, at one level I would have to agree. However, I would argue that if a competitor chokes, I can help him or her to take the experience, learn from it and then return even stronger. I would explore your thoughts, feelings and emotions, discuss factors leading up to choking and explain how coping mechanisms can be employed to deal with the situation. Essentially, I am suggesting that choking is okay. The key is dealing with it before it happens in future, or handling it if you suddenly feel it emerging. Nevertheless, my role is to provide a contingency plan for you to use if the situation goes too far. Choking can occur at any time during the race weekend and may happen during a race after a seemingly small mistake that has grown to a point where several small mistakes are perceived as being a total catastrophe.

Fatigue

Arguably, fatigue is more of a physical or physiological event that is beyond a competitor's control. Let's face it, if you are tired then you *are* tired! However, a consequence of fatigue may be a reduction, or indeed total loss, of attentional focus. Consider those race meetings where you have had to travel much further than usual, arrive late, and have to set up living accommodation or have difficulty finding the hotel or guest house. You get into the pit garage the following morning and experience major problems in keeping your concentration levels high. If you are able to identify fatigue as a factor in your performance, you can then deal with it appropriately. As I sit here now, I feel 'writer's fatigue' starting to come on, so I know that it is time for a break, otherwise my 'performance' will diminish. The chapter on relaxation may provide you with one way to overcome fatigue. Research in psychology has shown that a short, 'micro-sleep' is far more beneficial than trying to fight tiredness and keep going. The sport psychologist should attempt to help you plan for eventualities that may lead to fatigue and to provide windows of opportunity for you to recuperate wherever possible. I am sure you will have seen the motorway signs warning that 'tiredness kills, take a break'. While this is undoubtedly the case on public roads, it is equally possible on the racetrack. If you are ill prepared you must adjust your racing to suit the resources available to you. I will discuss fatigue in more detail in Chapter 6.

Motivation

Motivation is key to successful racing. If motivation levels are inadequate, attentional focus may be lost, or at the very least reduced. I will discuss motivation in depth in Chapter 3. Suffice to say, for now, motivation helps competitors to stay focused on the task in hand. If you are amongst a grid of high quality opponents, the challenge will help to keep motivation levels high.

If, on the other hand, you are guest-riding or driving for a team, where the other competitors are of a lesser standard, your motivation may drop. This is the classic David and Goliath scenario seen in sport, where the multi-million-dollar team gets beaten by the 'lowly' opposition. Pundits argue that this may be because the opposition played beyond their potential, the beaten team just couldn't get

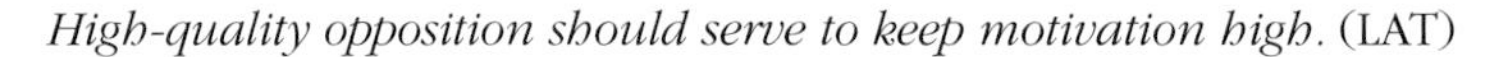

High-quality opposition should serve to keep motivation high. (LAT)

motivated, or a combination of the two. Nevertheless, motivation can act as an internal distractor and this should be borne in mind if lack of attentional focus becomes an issue.

External distractors

In contrast to internal distractors, external distractors are firmly located in the environment. They are provided by the sensory systems of the body. Humans have evolved as a visually dominant species. Forgive the pun, but we focus on visual input more than any other sense. In motorsport, as with sport in general, the auditory system is also a source of external distraction. I will discuss these below, before moving on to look at a certain kind of external distractor, 'gamesmanship', which manifests itself in so-called racing incidents and is effective in causing attentional focus to drop.

Visual distractors

Visual distractors can be found everywhere, and without training to overcome them are unavoidable. My office window overlooks the campus road, pathway and AstroTurf beyond. There are three opportunities for visual information to compete with my attentional focus every day. Cars, pedestrians, football and

The paddock is a busy place, fraught with distractions. (LAT)

hockey players use these facilities constantly, entering my field of vision and drawing my attention. I have trained myself to overcome this problem and instead focus on the task that I am working on at the time. Similarly, at the racetrack you will experience distractions in the form of sponsors, autograph hunters, well-wishers, media crews and the like, all competing for your attention and inadvertently preventing you from doing your job of racing. These factors will not change or go away. You should aim, therefore, to switch on and off from them as you choose. You will need to practise this. It does not just come easily.

Unfortunately, this situation does not change much when you are on the grid, or during the race. For example, as you enter Luffield and then the chicane before the start-finish straight at Silverstone, you pass several grandstand seating areas, usually full of spectators. Any of these areas can provide visual distractions. These may be different for different racers, but nevertheless, if you allow them into your attentional focus you may have less space for relevant and effective thought processes to take place. For example, you might focus on your racing all the way round the back of the circuit, only to have that 'I must look really good' thought as you enter the spectator areas. 'I must look really good' can then easily be followed by 'Oh no, I'm crashing'. A simple change in attentional focus can influence performance.

Pit boards are another bone of contention for me. I accept that they provide valuable information to the racer. Nevertheless, I always question why they are being used, what information is being displayed and what benefit is it to the competitor. Normally pit boards display position on track, lap time and perhaps distance from the competitor behind. I would argue that position on track is outcome-based (see Chapter 8 on goal setting) and is therefore detrimental to performance. I would argue that lap times are performance-based and are of some benefit but do not always improve performance. I would argue that distance from the competitor behind is not relevant, unless a large enough gap to back off a little is strategically beneficial. The main point I am making here is that I would expect you to be circling the track in search of that 'feeling' of flowing smoothly and quickly. All is going well, until you go past the pit wall, glance across at your pit board and get distracted by what it is telling you. It is ironic that the very thing put out to help you may in fact hinder you as you strive for the perfect lap. Again, I am not advocating throwing the pit board away, but I am advocating questioning what you do with the information and whether it affects your flow or not.

Auditory distractors

There are many noises that might be detrimental to attentional focus. Indeed, noises can put a racer off their focus very easily. The crowd would be an obvious example, although some racers say that they don't hear the crowd much, if at all. Imagine trying to run through a pre-performance routine on the starting grid while the crowd is cheering, air horns are sounding, the tannoy is running a commentary, and so on. When the lights have finally gone out and the race is under way, one might think that such distractions will disappear. However, although they may indeed reduce in number or volume, they do not always disappear. It may be that new distractors emerge. The obvious one is the noise made by an opponent's bike or car when they are right on your tail. The noise made by their exhaust and engine is basically shouting, 'I am right here!' This can cause you to focus on the opponent rather than on the track in front of you.

A less obvious example comes from a conversation I had with a motorcycle endurance racer at Donington Park. We had run through a mental imagery routine for him before the six-hour circuit race and he was confident in how this would inform his ride. When he came in after his first session on the bike he told me how he was focused on riding the circuit, the right-hander into Redgate, down the sweeping Craner Curves, tipping in through the Old Hairpin and under Starkey's Bridge, climbing the hill into McLean's and into Coppice. Then he told me how all of his attentional focus was 'destroyed' as he opened the throttle along Starkey's Straight. The thundering noise above his head from a commercial aeroplane was completely unexpected and off-putting. East Midlands Airport is very close to

You may unwittingly focus on opponents who are right on your tail. (Rimstock plc)

The straight at Donington Park is directly underneath the flight path of the local airport. (Author)

Donington Park and aeroplanes take off on such a regular basis that they are even included on the graphics in some computer racing games!

After discussing a strategy to filter out the noise as irrelevant to the racing that was taking place, the rider grew accustomed to the aerial activity very quickly and regained focus. In an endurance race this was less of an issue; however, if it had been a 25-lap circuit race, perhaps the distraction would have been enough for the leader to create an irretrievable gap. Nowadays I always incorporate an aeroplane into a mental imagery sequence for this circuit. The key is, yet again, to deal with the distractors, not to avoid them.

Gamesmanship

Gamesmanship is the use of strategic efforts to cause a distraction and ultimately affect concentration. Gamesmanship can be employed in different ways in an attempt to obtain the same result: loss of concentration. Ask yourself why a particular opponent always seems to be the last person to get into grid position. You have completed your warm-up lap and have stopped on the grid in your qualifying position. You then wait for what seems like an eternity while your rival holds everybody up until he or she is ready. This is an example of stalling for time, and they are, in fact, controlling their own pre-race routine. More importantly, they are controlling you. Next time, why not try the same thing? At the very least it should retain more heat in your tyres than your opponents who are waiting on the grid for you.

Intimidating or unnerving comments may also act as external distractors. Imagine how your focus could change if an opponent approached you before the race and told you: 'It's payback time for that move in the last race.' Suddenly your attention has moved to reflecting on the past instead of focusing on the present and on your own preparations.

Ironically, compliments can have a similar effect. If a fellow competitor has ever come over to you, saying how smoothly you go through a particular section of the circuit, you may take this as a compliment. However, be warned. This may be a psychological attempt to get you to think about this process, whereas before the comment you didn't need to think, you just did it. The next time you go through that section of track you will more than likely think about how well you go through ... and then go through it poorly. The message here is: do not allow any comments to disrupt your attentional focus in any way, shape or form. Be wise to what people tell you, listen to the comments, rise above them, evaluate and take them on board or dispense with them. You should be in control of what affects your performance!

Of course, I am not advocating the use of these distractors in order to put your opponents off. What I am doing is providing an insight into how you can protect

Try to control exactly when you take up a grid position. (Caterham Cars)

yourself mentally from undesirable tactics. However, we do not live in an ideal world. Teams have to please sponsors to avoid losing financial backing. The crowd must be entertained. Racers have to protect their contracts to avoid losing their livelihood or status. In order to accomplish these things, you should consider whether using these tactics sits comfortably with your conscience. Nevertheless, at least you are now aware of what may be taking place during race weekends.

Associative or dissociative strategies?

The human body provides a certain amount of information about a competitor's performance, so monitoring bodily activity can be extremely useful in providing information that may affect attentional focus. These strategies are particularly useful if a competitor is carrying an injury. There are numerous examples of racers who have competed with broken bones, ligament damage or muscular/tissue injury.

Attentional focus can be influenced depending on whether one uses an associative or dissociative strategy. An associative strategy is one in which the competitor monitors, and is fully aware of, what information his or her body is providing. For example, increased heart rate, any tension of the muscle groups, heavier or laboured respiration etc, all provide feedback on how the body is coping with the exertion. In contrast, a dissociative strategy is one in which the competitor blocks out information provided by the body. For example, the increasing pain in your shoulder from yesterday's crash is blocked out of conscious awareness by thinking about something else.

Generally in sport, different types of performer use associative and dissociative strategies in different ways. Evidence has shown that elite level performers in marathon running tend to use associative strategies, presumably as a way of measuring perceived fine changes in their physical and physiological state at any given moment. In this way the runner is able to feel the discomfort or pain signals, interpret them, and translate the information into a measure of performance that can be evaluated. Having evaluated the signals, the runner is then able to adjust his or her speed to suit the conditions. Non-elite performers, in contrast, have been shown to tend towards dissociative strategies. I would anticipate that this method is used as a way of ignoring the discomfort and pain. The last thing you would want is a constant reminder of how difficult the task is, especially if you still have 13 miles left to run. The same could be said about the intense pain in your wrist or ankle after a previous crash during practice. Dissociative strategies seem, therefore, to be an effective coping mechanism for this task. However, I would have to question whether running through the pain barrier is a good thing or whether it is, in fact, dangerous for the body.

In motorsport, I would find it difficult to suggest using an associative strategy for a competitor carrying an injury. I accept that such a strategy may provide information regarding how far to 'push it', but with the speeds involved and the potential implications of paying attention to one's bodily signals at 150mph gives

Practise associating with and dissociating from the signs of discomfort. (Author)

me cause for concern. The only exception to this would be as a way of monitoring perceived physical and physiological condition during an endurance race, but I would only recommend this at opportune moments, such as on a straight, uneventful section on the circuit.

For a non-injured competitor, the use of an associative strategy could be used temporarily, at similar points on the circuit, as a means of momentarily dipping in to assess 'How do I feel?' I would like to hope that the answer that comes back is 'I feel good ... I feel strong,' or something to that effect. We are now back in the realms of self-talk (Chapter 10). These positive phrases feed back to the 'racing brain', motivation levels remain buoyant, or rise, and the competitor stays on the pace. I'm sure you can see how useful this would be, especially in endurance racing.

Adopting a dissociative strategy, when carrying an injury, would seem to be an obvious choice. Of course, the doctor may have administered a cortisone injection to remove the pain. If not, why not administer a 'mental pain-killer' by blocking out the pain signals? By ignoring the signals and instead focusing on something else, such as the competitor in front, an injured competitor can continue beyond the pain barrier.

Let me give you a practical example of how this can be learned, by understanding the differences between the two strategies. Stand against a wall and begin to assume a sitting position, so that your back is pressing firmly against the wall with your knees bent, as if you are sitting on a chair. Now, focus on your legs. After a minute or two they will start to ache. Focus on the ache. This is an associative strategy. You are monitoring and are aware of the pain building in your legs. Stay in position, but now start to focus on anything other than the pain in your legs. Look outside and describe what you see aloud, or have a conversation with someone else in the room about the weather. You will notice that the pain seems to disappear. This is a dissociative strategy. Now return to the associative strategy and the pain will be quite unbearable after a few minutes. Before you stop, go back to the dissociative strategy once more. Almost as if by magic, the pain seems to disappear again. This example shows how you can accept or reject bodily information at your discretion. Practise this example until you become proficient at associating and dissociating. When you become proficient, you can move on to monitoring and rejecting other bodily sensations, such as heart rate and muscle tension. You can use the same technique to filter information in or out depending on your preferences.

I spoke above about employing an associative strategy to provide feedback about the body's physical and physiological condition, and how this can be used as a motivational tool through the use of positive self-talk statements. Interestingly, however, self-talk itself can also act as an internal distractor. If negative thoughts enter conscious awareness as self-talk statements, you may spend more time addressing these than focusing on more pertinent aspects of your racing. The important thing to consider is how the self-talk is influencing performance. If you tell me that it is distracting you, or diverting your attention in a negative way, I would seek to explore ways in which it can be adapted to suit your specific requirements in a more effective manner. Of course, you must always bear in mind the slim possibility that self-talk simply does not work for you. Let's face it, we all have preferences for types of food or forms of music. Why should psychological skills techniques be any different?

At this point, let us move on to discussing whether changes in physiological activation reflect changes in attentional focus, what role the nervous system plays in attentional focus, and how attentional skills can be assessed using alternative methods, before I provide advice on ways to develop, improve and refine attentional focus, and thus concentration.

Arousal, nerves and loss of attentional focus

As I have established in the sections above, the appraisal of both internal and external stimuli is an important aspect of attentional focus. From my experience in working with competitors at various levels I have found that arousal and nervousness may be interpreted as threats, and consequently individuals can become 'psyched out' by their perceived nervousness. As a result, attention may be lost, concentration reduced and performance affected. However, arousal and nervousness may alternatively be interpreted positively. If you think of your body as a finely tuned machine, in the same way that your race bike or car is finely tuned, the physiological signals reflect this state of fine-tuning. You are aware of whether or not your bike or car is working properly by interpreting the signs. You should also interpret the signs from your body in the same way. I like to use this 'fine-tuning' analogy in motorsport for obvious reasons. If you can hear and feel a misfire in your engine, then you should equally be able, with practice, to hear or feel a misfire in your own physiological state. By accessing physiological information, you should be providing useful information to help retain attentional focus.

You should be careful, however, not to spend too long focusing on these internal cues, because you may be missing what is happening externally. Your attentional focus should be constantly shifting in order to provide the greatest amount of information possible at any given moment.

The 'fight-or-flight' response

The body's autonomic nervous system is responsible for providing us with a survival mechanism in cases of danger. This is a remnant of our evolutionary past when we were required to fight or run in order to avoid being killed or eaten by predators. Obviously, nowadays there is little chance of us being eaten, unless we are very unlucky! Nevertheless, the body's response to threat remains with us – you will know this if you have inadvertently tripped on a flight of stairs or had a 'moment' out on track when everything suddenly went a little wayward. Your heart rate would have suddenly started racing, your pupils would have dilated and your palms may have gone sweaty. This is a natural reaction. Simply look at the eyes of a racer as soon as he or she has finished the race and you will see a 'wild' look; the 'fight-or-flight' response to danger.

With this in mind, I set out to examine the effects of driving on the heart rate during a session on track at Rockingham. In a pilot investigation to test the equipment, I wore a Polar heart rate monitor and transmitter, climbed aboard a Lotus Elise prepared by the Johnny Herbert Rockingham Experience, and set about pushing the envelope. My resting heart rate beforehand was around 70 beats per minute, which is a little higher than normal for me; my resting heart rate is more usually in the region of 60–65bpm, so the recorded baseline in the mid 70s indicates a raised level of physiological arousal. This was not surprising given

This wild look epitomises the fight-or-flight reaction to danger. (Rimstock plc)

the task ahead. Three points are worth mentioning here. At one point during the session I inadvertently began to lose rear-end grip. Believing I could regain control, I counter-steered – too much – and spun out. While this was unfolding, my heart rate went skywards and my autonomic nervous system went into 'fight-or-flight' mode, a natural evolutionary response to danger.

The purpose of explaining this is that in competitive motorsport you must be able to get back on the case as soon as possible. The adrenaline is pumping from the spin, but as a competitor you have to regain control of your faculties and concentrate quickly. Having established that the Polar equipment could be used to measure heart rate in a motorsport situation, I carried out some applied work with a racer in the British Superbike Championship in 2002. The aim was to measure heart rate during a championship race to see how it fluctuated as the race progressed and to see if sections of heart rate could be identified in relation to danger situations on track. The racer wore a Polar monitor inside his leathers and a transmitter around his chest. As was the case with my heart rate at Rockingham, the rider's resting heart rate was reasonably low, although the level of competition may have been elevating it to some extent.

Another point to note, in addition to cardiac deceleration in the figure opposite, is the small drop in heart rate approximately halfway through the race. This was linked to a strategic passing manoeuvre that was successfully executed. As the final lap drew to a close the rider, who was not under pressure from any opponents at this point, displayed reduced heart rate relative to the rest of the race. A small elevation in heart rate is evident as the rider stood on the podium taking applause, as is the length of time that the heart rate remained relatively high compared to previous baseline levels. This was possibly a result of elevated adrenalin levels in the body during this time.

Developing, improving and refining attentional focus

So far in this chapter I have discussed what attention is and how it relates to concentration. I have introduced the idea that attentional focus is not fixed but, rather, changes as conditions dictate. It is necessary to practise techniques aimed at retaining attentional focus long before the actual event. Shifting of attentional focus is not an easy thing to do unless you have practised it beforehand.

In the same way, you would not expect to explain how the clutch and gears move a vehicle and then see a beginner pull away smoothly, or carry out a controlled racing start on the first attempt. In practising for improved concentration you do not need to learn a new technique, beyond those described in this book. The key lies in using the techniques I discuss in chapters 8–11, so I will not go into them in detail here. You may, for example, use cue words or self-talk to provide a direction in which your attention should be guided: 'Watch him coming up on the inside at Coppice'; or, 'Block pass … shut the door'. Alternatively, you may set process or performance goals and need to evaluate these when you are on track, *ie* you are allocating resources to a particular task. You may establish so-called 'pre-performance' routines that come into play during race weekends, so that you know what you should be doing at different times, *ie* you are putting the spotlight onto one or several tasks requiring your attention. Essentially, you are filling your mind up with relevant things to do in order not to

Fluctuations in heart rate during a championship race meeting of British Superbikes, Donington Park 2002. (Boot-Handford/Author)

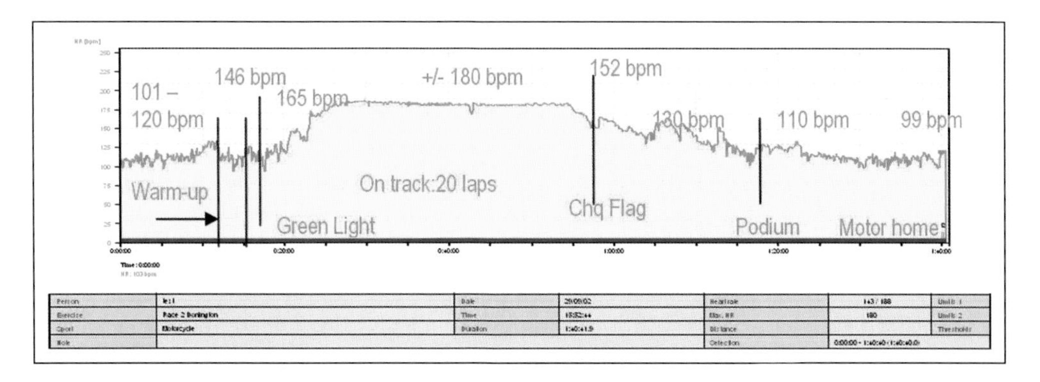

REACTION

OPPOSITE: *The Batak Wall has been used to train competitors to react swiftly to changes in the field of vision.* (Author)

become distracted when there is seemingly nothing to do. It seems far harder to distract somebody when they are focused on something than when they are not. Try having a conversation with your wife, husband or partner when they are engrossed in an activity. They appear not to be able to have a conversation, or if they do, it is usually minimal. My wife identifies with this comment every time she needs an answer from me when I happen to be writing. Alternatively, you may benefit from using mental imagery as a way to avoid distractions. Practise visualising a competition and gather evidence to plug into your mental image to enhance it.

In our Sport Psychology laboratory at the University of Worcester, we train athletes, drivers and riders in improving their reaction times, using our 'Batak Wall'. The Batak Wall consists of a set of nine lights that light up in random sequences. The participant is required to extinguish as many lights as possible and as quickly as possible in a period of time. After a minute or two, this becomes extremely tiring and reflects concentration and reactions to 'warning signals'. Drivers and riders can hone their reaction time skills using this equipment, and this skill can then be transferred to the track. Essentially we believe that the strengthened connections within the brain will allow you to react quicker when you need to.

Combine any of these techniques to achieve your aims, but also learn to avoid judgemental thinking. Judgemental thinking is the scourge of sport psychology. Competitors seem to be under the impression that any activity or performance or part of that performance should be judged, usually critically and harshly. The end result is usually negative and adversely influences future performance. If you have committed an error on lap 2, it does not mean that you should reflect on that error for the next ten laps, because if you do your performance will be poor. Deal with the fault, evaluate it (quickly under race circumstances) and then move on. It has happened – you can do nothing about it, but you can change it next time around. A mistake is not a mistake if you learn from it. As I say to my clients, experience comes from making mistakes ... what you are doing is acquiring experience.

Final comment

Attention and concentration are crucial to effective performance. If a competitor is not competent in switching attention, focusing and refocusing when things go awry, that is the place to start in developing the skill. The practical techniques can be used and refined to suit your own individual requirements. Use them in the same way that a tailor would use your measurements to make a bespoke suit. You can build a mental armour to cover any eventuality that you think may happen during your career.

Chapter 3

Motivation

Introduction

Motivation is an extremely complex psychological process that can spur racers on to sublime levels of performance. However, a lack of motivation may be blamed when a racer's performance drops to unacceptable levels. A racer may benefit from receiving a barracking from the team manager, so that he or she bucks their ideas up. But for some racers this may do more harm than good and may lead to even worse performances on track. So, how do you know what works for you? This chapter will explore the complex nature of motivation and provide some guidance on what to consider when motivating yourself or others.

What exactly *is* motivation?

If motivation is such a complex concept, it is little surprise to discover that defining it is not easy. However, for operational purposes there are several ways of regarding it. At a very general level, motivation is a state that drives us to act in a certain way. For instance, I am motivated to finish this chapter – but if you put a Lotus Elise and a track in front of me I won't even reach the end of this page! My motivation will have entirely changed.

Some people see motivation as little more than a physiological state of arousal. The more aroused or psyched up you are, the greater your motivation to compete. Yet, as I pointed out in the previous chapter, if you are too aroused your level of concentration will drop and your performance will dip. If this happens, I guarantee you will not be motivated.

However, these views of motivation may have some element of truth in them. If you are feeling extremely tired, lethargic and lacking in energy (a low state of physiological arousal), the last thing you would want to do is get out on track for a practice session. If, on the other hand, you feel full of energy you would probably relish the thought of one. Similarly, if everything is going well, psychologically speaking, you are more likely to want to get some more track time in.

RIGHT: *Motivation changes at the slightest opportunity.* (David.WillowPhotography.co.uk)

BELOW: *Do you compete for trophies and rewards?* (Caterham Cars)

Nevertheless, motivation is far more than either of these. It is based on several extra psychological factors, such as how highly you value your goals, your expectations, and possible conflicting motives. Sport psychologists differentiate between external and internal motivation, and these are important to the way racers think about their racing.

External or extrinsic motivation

Extrinsic motivation is the term applied to those people who race for external reasons. Your motivation comes from rewards or from other people. Ask yourself the question, 'Why do I race?' The question is trying to discover whether you race for rewards such as trophies, podiums, financial gain, fame and celebrity. I would not be surprised to hear that you race for trophies and podiums.

Mind you, I would question whether these motives are good, but I will leave that discussion until after I have outlined intrinsic motivation. If you race for extrinsic reasons, you will be spurred on by reward, and as long as you continue in a rich vein of good form the rewards will continue. However, when things go less successfully you will experience the flipside of reward – punishment. The consequences of your poor performance are usually negative, and although punishment may give you the kick up the backside that you need to get back on track, it is arguably amongst the best de-motivating practices you can experience. Moreover, rewards also begin to lose their reinforcing nature after a while and you will need greater rewards to satisfy the drive to succeed. Viewed in this way, rewards are rather like addictions, whereby the 'hit' needs to be more intense to gain the same amount of pleasure that was previously experienced.

Internal or intrinsic motivation

In contrast, intrinsic motivation comes from within. It is about fulfilment and satisfaction, or the desire to 'get it right'. In working with a racer, I ask the question, 'If all the trophies and rewards were taken away, would you still race?' If the answer is 'Yes', I am pleased that he or she is racing for the best reasons. Amongst the hardest things I have to do is ask racers *not* to race to win. They usually look at me with total bewilderment: 'Why is this guy asking me not to win?' In fact, I am not saying don't win. I am asking you to place emphasis on mastering your own racing technique so that it is *this* that provides satisfaction and fulfilment. Race to race; focus on the process of racing.

If you consider the process of how to put in a satisfying performance, rather than considering the outcome (which is beyond your control anyway), you will have a far better chance of winning. So if you race for intrinsic reasons, the trophies and podiums are likely to come as a side-effect or consequence of your intrinsic reasons for competing, which is to beat the best person on the circuit, yourself!

Always strive to improve on your previous performances. (Caterham Cars)

Some theories of motivation

One way to look at motivation is as being rather like a drive or urge, pushing us to achieve. When the drive diminishes, motivation is lost. Motivation may, therefore, be related to physiological arousal. If the body is sufficiently aroused, levels of motivation remain high. However, motivation may also be viewed in terms of being part of our personality, a personality trait. I might describe you as a highly motivated person, suggesting that you are motivated in many aspects of your life, not just in racing.

In the diagram below, motivation drives us to move through each stage of the pyramid until we reach the top. At the bottom of the pyramid, our priority is to satisfy basic survival needs and desires, such as obtaining food. We are then motivated to find shelter, before seeking approval from others and approval from ourselves until we reach the pinnacle of mastery termed 'self-actualisation'. Self-actualisation is like the Holy Grail. It is the place where a racer finds everything almost effortless. A 20-lap race seems like it is over in ten minutes. A training session in the gym or a winter road run is easy. An early morning cycle ride is simple.

Taking this idea further, people are motivated towards achieving competence and mastery in all areas of their lives. Attempts to master different circumstances help us to feel good about our ability as racers. We seek out challenges to prove our capability and personal competence. During training sessions on my road cycle I find myself hunting for hills just to prove that I can overcome the challenge of getting over the crest. In racing, you may seek the limit time and time again until you perfect the line through the corner – in the rain, on slicks when you should be on wets – just to prove to yourself that you are capable.

In contrast, if your attempts at mastery result in failure, your motivation will decrease and the negative, downward spiral of despair will emerge. The message for racers is clear: do not underestimate your personal competence. If you do, you are likely to prefer activities that fail to stretch you, and you will ultimately lose the motivation to continue racing. It is also important to pay attention to your feelings about your attempts at mastery. Regardless of whether you are successful in your attempt, does it make you feel positive or negative? If your performance is poor it is not necessarily a good thing to be overly critical, as this will combine with your negative feelings and help to demotivate you. Rather, you should reflect

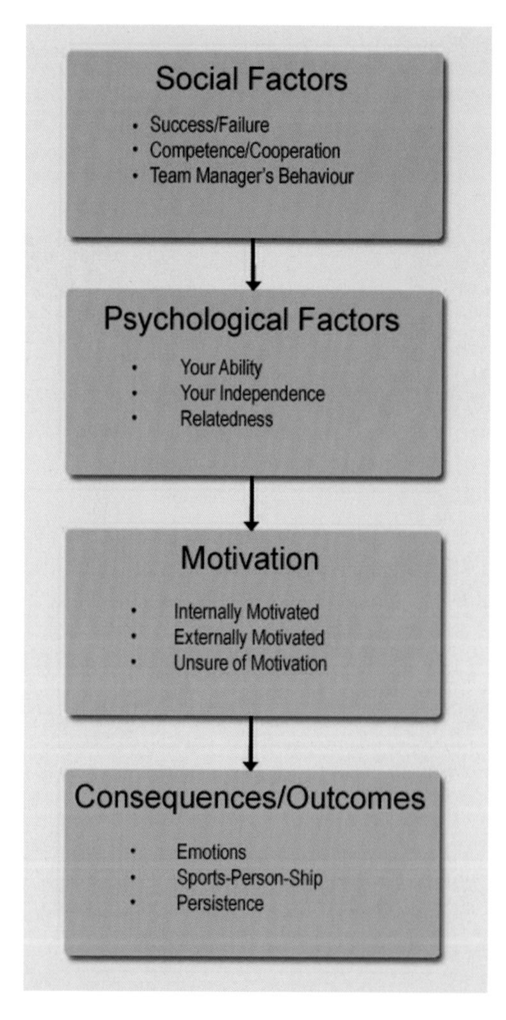

LEFT: *The components that impact on motivation.* (Boot-Handford/Author)

BELOW: *Racers are motivated to reach their full potential. Certain needs must be satisfied first.* (Boot-Handford/Author)

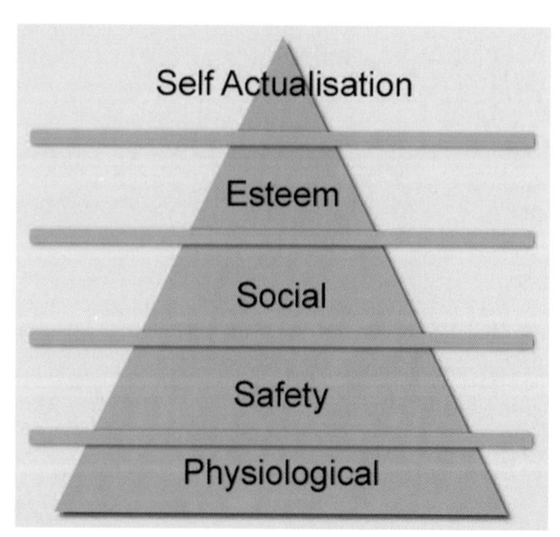

on why your performance was unsatisfactory and what the solution is to the challenge.

What factors influence motivation?

According to the schematic diagram opposite, there are four components that make up our motivation in motorsport: social factors; psychological mediators; underlying motivation; and perceived outcomes. I will cover each of these in turn to build a usable picture for racers.

Social factors

Social factors play an important role in motivating racers but I am not convinced that they are fully aware of this. The need to achieve success is motivating in itself. However, you may adopt the opposite position, being motivated to avoid failure. I would always ask you to think differently about success and failure. Negativity should be pounced on and discarded. The behaviour of other people in the race team will undoubtedly influence your own behaviour and, ultimately, your motivation.

Other people may influence your motivation in a positive or negative way. (LAT)

A sport psychologist might consider observing and evaluating how the team functions around the racer, what issues emerge and how they are dealt with. If you are racing in a two-bike or two-car team, are there any team orders, and are the spare parts allocated equally to both racers in the team? I have known this not to be the case, and this has affected a racer's motivation because of the apparent lack of fairness.

Psychological mediators

Social factors inevitably influence a racer's psychological state. It is not necessarily the reality of those social factors that is significant, but rather the racer's perception of the situation. Your perception of your competence comes partly from social factors. I discuss issues relating to self-confidence in the next chapter so will not cover it here; suffice it to say, however, that if you have a poor perception of your competence, this will undoubtedly influence your motivational state in a negative way. Ideally you should strive for autonomy or independence.

By controlling how you improve the way that you race you will be competing for intrinsic or internal reasons rather than external rewards. The danger in competing for external rewards is that if they were to be taken away, perhaps due to poor performance, then levels of motivation would also inevitably diminish. My advice would perhaps focus on helping you to enhance your perceptions of competence and autonomy, by offering guidance on identifying the positives that show you are capable and 'could do this with your eyes shut' – metaphorically

If your perception of your own competence is high, your motivation levels are likely to remain strong. (David.WillowPhotography.co.uk)

Congratulate yourself for a job well done. (LAT)

speaking, of course. Racing with your eyes shut is never recommended ... unless, of course, you are Billy Baxter, attempting a lap of Donington Park in a World Record Attempt to be the fastest blind person to lap the circuit (Round 12, British Superbikes, 23 September 2007).

Motivation

I discussed intrinsic and extrinsic motivation at the beginning of this chapter and so will not go into it at length here. In terms of the flow diagram, however, social and psychological factors influence a racer's motivation to varying degrees, and this is linked to the type of motivation they hold. Of course, if you consider that you are an extrinsically motivated person then my role would perhaps involve trying to assist you in moving towards a more intrinsic focus, so that the potential pitfalls are fewer and possibly easier to overcome. If a racer is demotivated, this means that they show no real preference. It does not mean that they have no motivation. Instead it means that they have lost sight of why they race. Demotivation might indicate a slide towards the racer quitting their sport. Ask yourself the question again, 'Why do I race?' If you don't know what motivates you, how can you set goals, achieve those goals and progress beyond them? If you are unable to answer the question, don't panic. The simple solution is to start setting goals for yourself so that you can get back on route to racing.

Consequences/outcomes

Now we arrive at perhaps the most important aspect of motivation, the outcome or consequence of your behaviour. If social factors and perceptions are positive and intrinsic motivation is high, there is a good likelihood that outcomes will also be positive. Emotions are likely to be positive. If you have had a good race, you might feel elated. This feeling plugs directly back into your feedback mechanism, telling your brain that you are competent, you are in control and you can pull out all the stops when you need to. Positive emotion is a way of telling the rational, cognitive part of your brain that things feel good.

This is vital for me, because I believe that the key to successful performance lies in the process and how it feels, rather than the outcome. You will hear me say this time and again throughout this book. If you feel good about your performance, issues of sportsmanship – or, to be politically correct, sportspersonship – will be less important. Racing incidents or dangerous manoeuvres made by other competitors will not detract, or indeed distract you from achieving your goals in the race. You will be more inclined to brush these things aside, in the knowledge that despite such minor irritations, you can still do the business. Those competitors who can be heard vociferously berating others for their actions on track are already beginning to direct their motivation in the wrong place. Look around at the next race meeting and you will be able to identify this type of behaviour.

Highly motivated racers are more likely to be persistent. Nothing will stop them from achieving their goals. An excellent example here is the persistence displayed by Troy Bayliss during the 2002 World Superbike Season, where he crashed three times during the wet race at Silverstone, picked the bike up, and continued to finish a creditable fifth overall. As soon as motivation levels tail off, persistence is perhaps one of the first things to suffer. That feeling of not wanting to go to the gym for the twice-weekly workout, or of not wishing to put the effort in during tyre testing sessions or during winter testing, may also indicate motivation levels tailing off. As I have explained above, by focusing on the process rather than the outcome motivation levels will last for longer. If they begin to tail off, you should perhaps look at your goals and decide whether to change them so that you can return to successful racing.

The 'Dopamine Hit'

I will discuss this topic in more detail in Chapter 7, on the brain's reward system. For now, however, it is important to point out that racers will receive a physiological 'hit', rather like an addictive reward, for successful performances.

Having received this reward, we strive to seek out the pleasurable sensation again and again. This is perhaps why sexual desires are so strong in humankind. The physiological change in brain chemistry is in itself a highly motivating experience and is one that helps to maintain motivational levels, but *only* for as long as it continues to be experienced. As discussed earlier, I would not suggest that your only reason for racing should be to satisfy potentially addictive cravings, but it does offer a satisfying feeling when you can get it!

Developing motivation

The sport psychologists Weinberg and Gould provide a useful set of guidelines for teachers, coaches and trainers to assist in building motivation. I will interpret these guidelines for motorsport and deal with each one below.

Situational and personal factors in motivation

Personal factors interact with the situations in which racers find themselves. For example, you may have had a bad accident at a particular circuit before and really don't relish the thought of having to race there this season. On the flipside, you

A bad accident may influence your motivation to compete at a particular circuit.
(David.WillowPhotography.co.uk)

may have won the race there last year and are therefore highly motivated to do well again. Alternatively, the family pet may have died and this has left you upset and traumatised.

It is important to establish how much these factors are influencing your motivation to compete or succeed. Your progress is only possible if you have a strong foundation. In exploring situational and personal factors, it is possible to create this foundation.

Appropriate feedback in motivation

It is important for racers to provide appropriate feedback when reflecting on their performances. This links directly with the way in which people assess their performance. If a racer is not performing optimally, perhaps as a result of illness or recovery from illness, they should not expect to perform as well as when they are in peak condition. Yet time and time again I hear the despair in their voices because they are attributing a less than successful performance to lack of ability when physical condition is the culprit. The next time you have a cold or flu, for example, assess your driving or riding on a journey to the shopping mall. You will not feel as alive as when you are 100 per cent fit. So why should it be any different when you are racing after an illness or injury? It is important, therefore, to monitor whether you are assessing your performance appropriately in light of

Use evidence to motivate you when necessary. (LAT)

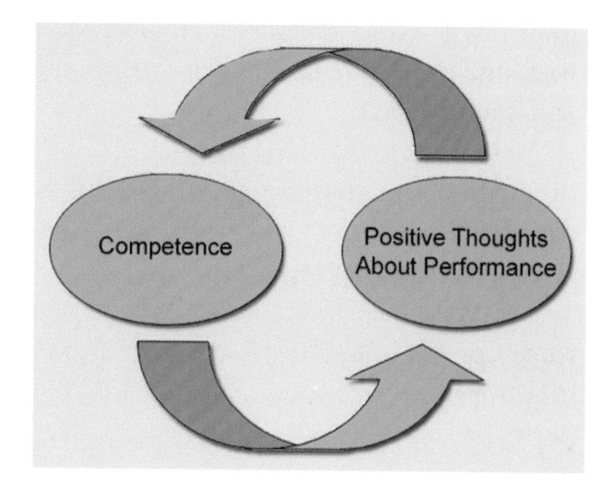

Competence and positive thinking are both linked to motivation. (Boot-Handford/Author)

these judgements, and correct any misperceptions. Use hard evidence from datalogging, lap times, tyre wear etc to help you make an informed assessment of how you are doing under the circumstances.

Perceived competence or ability and motivation

Providing appropriate feedback is an important way of influencing your perceived competence. If a racer monitors and reflects on his or her performances, searching for and picking out positive information, they will feel a heightened sense of competence: 'I can do this because I am a successful racer.' This becomes self-perpetuating, feeding back into itself rather like a loop. Competence leads to positive thoughts about your performance, which leads to a feeling of competence, which leads to positive thoughts about your performance, which leads to competence etc. If you are competent, you are more likely to be in control of the situation and your motivation will remain high.

Process goals in motivation

As I have pointed out elsewhere in this and other chapters, focusing on the outcome is not necessarily the best approach to adopt. Process or mastery of the task is, in my opinion, more important. If I can help a racer to master their technique and set out to beat him- or herself, or the circuit, they should be more of a threat to opponents than if they set out to win. There is no control in winning. Everyone else is trying to do the same thing and it is not possible to control their race, only to influence it. If the racer focuses on mastery of performance instead of outcome, then other competitors will more than likely get sucked into strategy, and can then be controlled to a greater extent. It is almost as if he or she is competing in a different competition to everyone else, playing by his or her own rules and racing for a different purpose; which, of course, they are! If you sit and think this argument through it makes perfect sense. Yet few people adopt it as a strategy.

Professor Duda, an expert in sport-motivation from the University of Birmingham, suggests that people can help to enhance their level of involvement in a task in a number of ways. These can be adopted in motorsport and I have adapted some of them in the table below. You may use these strategies when thinking about ways to increase your level of motivation in racing.

What is the situation? (Situational structure)	What should I do about it? (Strategies)
I am finding it difficult to achieve (Task attainment)	Use SMART goal setting (see Chapter 8). Make the demands of the task individualised and specific to each racer.
I am unsure about how much control I have in what happens (Authority)	Racer to take responsibility for their own professional development. Racer to be actively involved in decision-making process.
I am not being given accurate and honest recognition for my achievement (Recognition)	Recognise individual progression and effort. Team briefings to recognise progress. Provide equal opportunities in two-racer teams.
Grouping	Not applicable to motorsport.
I don't know whether I am making progress or whether my standard of racing is acceptable (Evaluation and standards)	Develop evaluation criteria related to goals set. Racer to provide self-evaluation. Ensure consistency and meaningfulness.
I am expected to deliver when testing has been limited (Appropriateness of Timing)	Provide adequate time to develop skill or progress to next task. Assist racer in establishing training/competition schedules.

Concluding remarks

I have introduced the concept of motivation as being vital to all areas of one's life, let alone racing. Without motivation we would fail miserably. Without motivation there would be little reason to get out of bed in the morning for work. However, at some point many if not all of us experience dips in motivation, which, if left unattended, grow increasingly larger and more distinct. When motivation is high, nothing stops us. We set out to do something and we strive towards achieving that goal. The goal itself should be carefully devised and should, I would argue, be related to mastery of a task rather than its outcome. Strategies can be put into place to ensure that motivation levels are established or retained, and control over situational and personal factors will help to do this. Motivation is also linked with self-confidence and self-esteem, which are the focus of Chapter 4.

Chapter 4

Self-confidence and self-esteem

Introduction

Self-confidence is that elusive, magical ingredient that gives us supremacy over our thoughts, actions and, ultimately, our performances. When self-confidence is high, it seems that nobody else on the circuit can even come close to beating us. In contrast, when self-confidence is low our racing world seems to fall apart. Nothing goes right. Everybody else seems so much better than we are. As I explain in Chapter 5, on stress, this leads to a damaging downward spiral that is perceived as irretrievable. All it takes, however, is that one race where things pick up and self-confidence starts to return. In this chapter I shall explain the elements that contribute to self-confidence, provide ways of identifying the symptoms associated with low self-confidence, and provide guidance on overcoming the situation.

What is self-confidence?

Self-confidence is a difficult concept to define. It is an expectation about achieving success. It should, however, be a realistic expectation. Over-confidence in a racer's ability can be as damaging as under-confidence. The key is finding your own peak and staying there for as long as possible. So self-confidence is not something that one either has or does not have. We all have a certain level of self-confidence all of the time, but we may need to increase or reduce it to arrive at an optimal level for performance.

Self-confidence can be viewed in two ways. You might be a confident person in all kinds of situations, whether this is in racing, in your career, or in your social life. Alternatively, you might be a confident person in particular situations and not in others. For example, if you are confident in racing at club level and then decide to step up a level next season, you may find that your confidence falls away as you sit on the grid for the first race of the new season. The specific situation causes you to doubt yourself and your confidence goes down as a result.

The schematic diagram below provides a useful framework for me to explain how self-confidence may affect a racer mentally. The key to this diagram is the extent to which competitors believe in their ability to be successful.

Different racers perceive the reality of a situation in different ways. It is how we interpret the signals of a situation that is important. The event remains the same. The circuit remains the same length and has the same corners. If it rains, it rains for every competitor. The racer brings to this event his or her general level of self-confidence and attitude to racing ('Am I confident in all situations?'). This is complemented by the racer's level of self-confidence for this particular race at this moment in time. It might be the case that you are confident in all situations but find that you are suddenly not feeling confident *now*. Alternatively, it might be that you are not generally a confident person, but today you are feeling so good and so confident that nothing can stop you. So, ask yourself the question, 'Am I confident in *this* situation?' How you answer this question will have an influence on how well you perform in the race. Your actual performance may be positive or negative depending on how confident you are up to the chequered flag.

The killer blow to self-confidence is dealt with when you ask the question, 'What does it mean for me?' Humans simply love to compare themselves with and evaluate themselves against others. Arguably, in competitive motorsport this is taken to extremes: 'I want to be the fastest, latest on the brakes, quickest through the corners,' etc. The tools we use to evaluate ourselves against others are success, satisfaction and perceived causes of failure. A racer's perception of success is

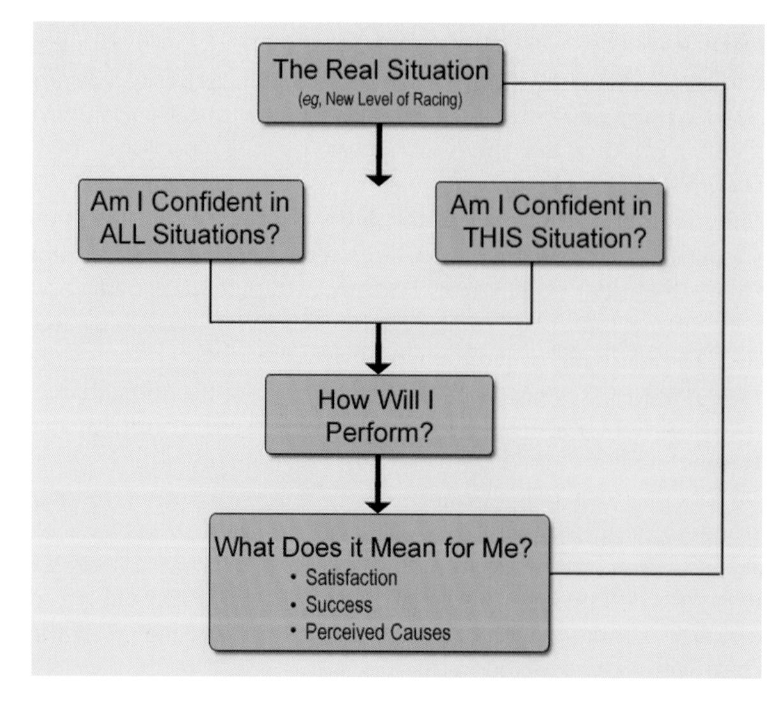

Identifying self-confidence in motorsport. (Boot-Handford/Author)

usually driven by outcomes: 'If I didn't win, I failed.' Satisfaction is linked closely with success: 'I am not satisfied because I did not win.' As I will point out repeatedly, neither of these thoughts is very productive nor, indeed, even appropriate, and I would challenge racers to question them. Yes, winning is important. Of course it is, otherwise why are we racing? Nevertheless, success and satisfaction feed back into our self-confidence and fuel it, or destroy it, for the next race. How many times has race two gone pear-shaped because you lost confidence after race one? There are better ways of using psychology to help your racing, rather than using it to hinder your racing.

After race one look at the possible reasons for your performance, and I do mean reasons, *not* excuses! If it was a good performance, you will focus on the positives, take the glory, and move forward with heightened self-confidence. However, if it was a poor performance you probably look for and magnify the negatives, while ignoring or minimising the positives. This will more than likely lead to feelings of negativity and may cause you to question your own ability. How irrational can this be? You have improved from your early days in racing. You have the potential, the capability, the skills, the motivation and everything else that constitutes a successful racer. Yet here you are, questioning yourself when you should be focusing on *how* to achieve your goals. Once self-confidence takes a dive it is difficult, although not insurmountable, to retrieve it. So if you have a poor performance you should still look for the positives, however small these may appear to be.

Over-confidence is equally harmful. Over-confidence occurs when a racer's confidence does not match the reality of their capabilities. If you do not possess the skills to do the things you believe you can do, you *will* fail. Of course, this is not to say that you may be unable to achieve a respectable level of competence at some point in the future, you just cannot do so right now. Psychologically, I believe that I am as strong as Michael Schumacher or Valentino Rossi. On a racetrack, either of these people would wipe the floor with me, without even getting out of bed! My race-craft is nowhere near the expertise of such men. So it is my physical capability that holds me back, and my psychological expertise could lead to over-confidence.

However, over-confidence tends not to last too long, since the reality of constantly performing poorly will tug at the conscience of even the thickest-skinned person.

Lack of self-confidence is sometimes disguised so that the outside world is not aware of the true situation. For example, a racer who lacks self-confidence may compensate by acting in a confident manner. This false confidence usually manifests itself as arrogance and pretentiousness but is in fact a form of over-confidence. Returning to my earlier comment about perceiving situations realistically, the racer who experiences false confidence is misinterpreting the signs from the situation and needs to refocus his or her efforts to tune in to the *right* signs, the signs that will provide solutions.

Strategies for enhancing self-confidence

If a racer's self-confidence is under-developed or has deteriorated, it is necessary to raise or restore it. The first port of call would perhaps be to consider your self-confidence in specific situations. Psychologist Albert Bandura talks about self-confidence in specific situations and suggests that we look at four related elements: performance accomplishments; vicarious experience; verbal persuasion; and physiological arousal. Let us take a look at how each of these relates to racing.

Performance accomplishments: assess your performance

Capability is partially determined by previous accomplishments. Self-confidence is increased if previous performances were successful. It suggests that mastery of racing skills is taking place and progress is being made. In contrast, self-confidence is reduced if previous accomplishments have been poor. You should identify even the smallest improvements within a session on track. By doing this, you will elevate its importance in your mind and will feel good. For example, if you have negotiated one corner correctly out of the nine on a particular track, then give yourself a mental pat on the back for having got that corner sorted out.

The next challenge is to learn how to sort out another corner, and then another, until you have achieved the ideal lap. By focusing your efforts on the task, I

When you have resolved the challenge at one corner, do the same for the next one until you are successful in each sector. (Caterham Cars)

would expect your self-confidence to rise, even if only a little. The smallest increase is better than spiralling further downwards.

Vicarious experience: learning from others

Vicarious experience is learning through watching others perform a task. If a racer does not know which is the most effective line to take through a corner, he or she might benefit from watching an experienced racer go through that section in order to evaluate their technique. Of course, this works in another way too. If a racer knows that they are quick and smooth through the section, this information confirms their capability and feeds back into their self-confidence.

Verbal persuasion: providing encouragement

Confidence can be boosted through the use of encouraging statements and comments made by other people. In sport, coaches or trainers usually occupy this role. In motorsport, the role may be filled by the team manager, the racer's family or team personnel. In motorsport especially, not enough positive feedback is handed out when things are going well. This may be because the sole focus of attention is usually only on first place on the podium. Anything less is failure. Not so! A good performance with a so-called 'poor' final position is not necessarily a failure if it means that the racer has gained knowledge and experience for future use. By focusing on developing your technique, your confidence to win the race will also develop.

An important point to consider is the expertise and kudos of the person who assumes the responsibility of providing encouragement, or who is chosen by the racer. If he or she has extensive experience there is more likelihood that the racer will believe and accept the comments being given. For example, few if any racers will pay much attention to the comments made by a spectator regarding how quickly the racer was going. However, if someone like Rubens Barrichello made the same comment, the racer would be far more inclined to take the feedback on board and use it as a confidence booster. This is exactly why it is important for racers to have the right kind of personnel around them during race weekends. The simple message here is to use verbal persuasion to your advantage but do not fool yourself with comments that you know you don't believe. I would see Michael Schumacher's consultancy role with Ferrari during the 2007 season as serving this purpose. The media may have speculated on the reasons for his presence at F1 circuits, but boosting the confidence of the team drivers was perhaps one of the most likely explanations.

Verbal persuasion can also be used in a darker way. The opponent who comes to you before a race, telling you, 'The way you go into bend number 1 is ever so strange, but you are fast there,' may be employing a distracting tactic that compels you to analyse exactly *how* you go through the corner. As you try to analyse yourself the next time into the corner, it will more than likely go wrong. There is a simple solution, however. When someone makes a comment like this you simply brush it aside as an attempt to psyche you out, and instead, with practice, you substitute a comment of your own.

Another type of verbal persuasion is self-talk, which is literally talking to yourself. I discuss how to use self-talk in detail in Chapter 10. However, in terms of self-confidence, self-talk is an excellent way of building and retaining positive thoughts throughout a race weekend. It will also help you to evaluate ongoing performance, so it provides a focus for your thoughts. Self-confidence is boosted by constructive comment. When you are out on track there is nobody to provide verbal feedback so it becomes necessary for you to provide the feedback yourself.

By focusing on the process rather than the outcome you will improve the way you negotiate the circuit every time you complete a lap. You should then feed this information back into your 'racing brain' and praise yourself where it will give maximum impact.

A comment on visual persuasion: pit boards

Although pit board information is not strictly 'verbal persuasion', because it contains visual information, I think it is necessary to bring it in at this point. The visual information is converted almost immediately into verbal, self-talk-like comment every time a racer sees it on the pit wall. It goes without saying that pit board information is important. There are no hard-and-fast rules on exactly what information should be displayed. You may have a personal preference for the type of information that you like to see on it, since it is important to ensure that the information provided is useful to your race. Typical information includes: number of laps remaining; lap times; distance from person behind; and position in race. Self-confidence will normally increase or remain at a high level if the information is suggesting that you are going faster or performing consistently.

There is, however, one point to bear in mind: why do you *need* the information that is being displayed? I would question a racer's use of some of the information that they ask for, on the grounds that it may serve to distract rather than assist them. See the section on visual distractors in Chapter 2 for further discussion of this point. The key factor is to ensure that the information displayed is used to enhance your performance.

With psychological support, you will not become disheartened if the pit board information begins to seem negative, but will instead be motivated to 'dig deeper' but remain focused.

Physiological arousal

Physiological arousal is not as much a predictor of self-confidence as the other three elements outlined above and a discussion here will not provide many benefits to the racer. Chapter 5 provides a more useful focus of attention for understanding how arousal influences the way in which we think. Suffice it to say

Ask yourself whether the information provided on your pit board is useful to you.
(David.WillowPhotography.co.uk)

that it is how you interpret the signs from your body that influences your expectations about your performance. For example, if you are sitting on the starting grid and notice that you have sweaty palms and your heart rate has gone up, you may interpret these signs as indicators of anxiety and your self-confidence will start to fade away. Yet if you interpret the same signs as indicators of excitement and readiness, your self-confidence will remain high.

Each of Bandura's elements influences our expectations about our performances, helping to provide feedback about our capability and to aid self-confidence. If capability and self-confidence are high then the expectation to race successfully also increases. A quote by Rainer Martens sums this up nicely: 'The most significant confidence for athletes is confidence in their ability … both physical and psychological' (Martens, 1987, p.155). This suggests that confidence can be viewed in terms of acquiring physical skills and techniques; acquiring psychological skills, such as mental imagery or self-talk; level of physical fitness for racing; and confidence in possessing suitable perceptual skills, such as good decision-making and adapting to ever-changing circumstances that occur in racing, on a race-to-race, lap-to-lap, or even second-to-second basis.

What are the symptoms associated with reduced self-confidence and how can you overcome them?

In working with a racer, one of my early questions is, 'Tell me about a race where everything seemed to go wrong.' This is designed to tease out which aspect of self-confidence he or she feels is a problem. I can use this as an exercise in showing that perhaps not all aspects of the racer's self-confidence are as damaged as he or she might think, especially when I follow with, 'Tell me about a race where everything seemed to go well.'

It is vital to be aware of the symptoms associated with diminishing self-confidence. Without such knowledge it is not possible to put strategies and procedures in place in order to change things. However, identifying symptoms is not an exact science and everybody is different. Nevertheless, I have compiled a list of possible symptoms below that may provide clues to emerging or present self-confidence issues.

Negative emotions

Racers lacking in self-confidence may show signs of negative emotions. If this happens look for signs of tension and anxiety, which may also be present. They may seem miserable all of the time or for no apparent reason. Positive emotion is associated with a relaxed state of body and mind and allows racers to assert themselves at critical moments in a race where the outcome could go either way.

Reduced concentration

Racers lacking in self-confidence may show signs of not concentrating or focusing on the task at hand. Other issues are clouding their judgement and worry takes a predominant role. Obviously, it is not possible to 'see' thought processes. Nevertheless, the signs are there. If the racer needs reminding of important information, or seems distracted by the plethora of people or activities going on around them, they may be lacking in concentration, which in turn may be

Identify the symptoms of reduced self-confidence and put a solution in place. (Caterham Cars)

influenced by a lack of self-confidence. This highlights the interaction between many of the topics discussed in this book and how it is crucial to be able to identify signs and symptoms in order to implement effective interventions.

Reduced effort

The effort a racer puts into his or her preparation for racing is also linked to confidence. If confidence is at an optimal level, effort tends to increase. I have spoken to racers who have given up trying midway through a race because they had no way of winning. My response to this is usually along the lines of 'You should be racing against yourself,' *ie* going out there to be better than you were previously. How else are you going to improve? Even in a race where the outcome is not going to see you on the podium, I would still expect you to put the effort in to push yourself. If the racer seems not to be too fussed about putting effort in, they may – and I stress, only *may* – have self-confidence issues to resolve. Of course, there could be any number of other reasons and these would need to be explored systematically.

Inappropriate goals

People who are lacking in self-confidence have a tendency to set goals that are easy to achieve, or set no goals at all. In either of these instances, there is no way that they can fail. If your goal is within easy reach, how can you expect to push the envelope and increase in competence? Ask yourself objectively whether your goals are realistic, yet challenging. If they are not, you need to consider expanding them to give yourself a fighting chance. Can you improve on your lap time simply because you have set your sights too low? If the goals set are questionable, then the racer may be disguising lack of self-confidence by means of easily achievable outcomes.

Inappropriate race strategies

In sport, competitors tend to adopt one of two types of strategy: play to win, or play not to lose. If a racer lacks self-confidence, he or she will be more inclined to adopt the latter of these strategies. They will protect lines, adopt a defensive racing style and not race the way that they would if confidence was high. A concern will be about making mistakes and, as I hope you would expect me to say, thinking about making mistakes places emphasis on making them and that is precisely what *will* happen. Ask yourself whether you are racing to win or racing not to lose. If you are racing not to lose, you will then need to ask yourself why you are thinking in this way. You may need to change your race strategy. The chapters on goal setting and self-talk provide comprehensive guidance on this.

Interrupted momentum

Everything in a race is running smoothly and according to plan when suddenly, the very next moment, it all seems to fall apart – in other words, the momentum has gone. A self-confident racer will overcome this with a never-say-die attitude and will bounce back during the race; but a racer who lacks self-confidence will find this an extremely difficult, if not impossible, task. I would ask a racer to identify whether they have ever experienced this situation and would perhaps suggest that goal setting would be an ideal way to keep the mind focused on the challenge rather than their apparent misperception of the situation. If your momentum is interrupted you will be less likely to enter 'the zone', where everything seems so easy.

Summary on assessing and improving self-confidence

By answering the questions below you will gain an insight into your own perceived self-confidence. It is important that you provide honest answers, so that you can move forward and develop further.

When am I over-confident?
When do I experience self-doubt?
Is my confidence consistent during the race (weekend)?
How do I recover from errors?
Am I indecisive or defensive in certain racing situations?
How do I respond to adversity?
Do I relish the prospect of and enjoy tough, highly competitive races?

Entering 'the zone' requires uninterrupted psychological momentum. (Centurion Racing)

Improving self-confidence is not as difficult as it may at first appear. The key is to consider what psychologists call 'process', leaving 'outcome' as a side-effect.

Process	Focusing on *how* to do something
Outcome	Focusing on the end result

In working with a racer, one of the first things I may do is to work through a mental imagery programme (see Chapter 11). By doing this, the racer can learn to visualise him- or herself performing successfully in the race. With practice, this visualisation simulates what happens in the race, strengthening connections in the brain so that split-second reactions and decisions are easier to make out on the real circuit. The old adage of 'practice makes perfect' should be used when you are honing your mental skills. So, if you visualise negotiating the circuit consistently over and over again, your visualised performance will get stronger and stronger. When you do the same thing in reality your performances will increase your self-confidence.

If mental imagery and goal setting are combined, there is no reason why a racer's thought processes will not improve. If he or she begins to think positively and confidently, then they will begin to act confidently. Let me provide a day-to-day example. I would like you to start smiling and begin to laugh. Laugh a little louder. How do you feel? I would expect you to be feeling rather happier and more positive than you did a moment ago. The same principle applies to self-confidence. If you act confidently you will feel confident, as long as you also have the capability for the task in hand. Change the way you think and you will change the way you act. The key, as I said earlier, is to be realistic about your ability. You should also set yourself achievable yet challenging goals.

Physical fitness is another key to improving self-confidence. If you have the stamina and mental endurance to match your physical capabilities, there is no reason why self-confidence should not be high. If you acknowledge that your physical fitness is lacking, then embark on a training programme or seek help from a fitness instructor to improve this area of potential weakness. When everyone else on the circuit is beginning to capitulate to the heat or the physical punishment of the race, you will step up a gear mentally and race at an improved psychological level. Potentially, your opponents are beaten before they leave the starting grid, in the same way that some boxers have their opponent beaten before putting one foot in the ring.

Ritual or routine?

Implementing what sport psychologists call a pre-performance routine is another way of improving self-confidence. Some people talk more in terms of 'ritual'. Valentino Rossi is known to adjust his 'delicate areas' and pull his leathers out from his bottom as he leaves the pit lane. Some people might argue that this is a

Physical fitness will compliment your psychological fitness. (RenaultF1)

ritual, but I would prefer to talk in terms of things that he does as a routine before racing – everything has been considered and is ready. Forget about 'lucky pants'. It is more important to know that you are wearing pants, that they are clean and that they are comfortable! Routines provide racers with ultimate control. For example, if a racer establishes a structured plan or strategy for a race weekend then they will know what to do, when, and for how long before each critical moment. It is important to establish routines, to provide a sense of security and familiarity. Without a structured regime uncertainty may creep in to the mind and wreak havoc on self-confidence.

Chapter 5

Emotion, anxiety and stress

COMPETITIVE PERFORMANCE is influenced, as indeed are all aspects of a person's daily life, by emotional states, mood and responses to stressful events. In this chapter I will discuss the effects of emotion, mood states and stress on performance in competition. The good news is that these bodily states can be identified and changed so that they are no longer cause for concern. I will explore ways of thinking about these states so that they do not interfere with performance. With practice, such states can even be used to enhance performance. In Chapter 10, on self-talk and cognitive restructuring, I outline how negative thoughts can adversely influence performance. I also show how these thoughts can be substituted with positive thoughts. The same technique can be used to identify emotional and mood states. It simply involves identifying the symptoms that seem to be causing a drop in performance and then dealing with them through cognitions, *ie* the way you think about these symptoms.

How do emotions and mood affect performance?

Everyone experiences emotions during daily life. Indeed, emotion and cognition, or thought processing, are inextricably linked. It is not possible to have one without the other. As you sit on the starting grid, you may feel happy and excited or nervous and uptight. How you feel will always influence the reality of the start. If you feel preoccupied your focus will be taken away from the job at hand. If you are feeling positive it will more often than not work in your favour and you will head into the first turn feeling pleased after the lights have gone out and the pack begins to move.

So, emotion can be thought of as experiencing feelings of joy, fear, anger and interest, as well as threat, sadness and disgust. Emotions are also multi-faceted, in that they can be subjective, biological, social or purposeful in nature. The subjective experience of emotion is 'how does the emotion make me feel?' Biologically, the same question applies, but this is linked to how you feel

Emotions may influence your performance. (David.WillowPhotography.co.uk)

physiologically rather than psychologically. For example, how you interpret the sudden increase in heart rate you have just experienced considers emotion from a biological viewpoint. Socially, emotion is the visual signal of the emotional state you wish to display to the world. A racer may portray body language suggesting contentment, happiness and interest in the journalist or camera crew interviewing him or her, but may be feeling threatened by their questioning about recent poor performances. Emotion is linked directly to motivation and was covered in Chapter 3.

You might be forgiven for thinking that the term 'emotion' has almost negative connotations. It suggests that rational thought is being displaced by irrational thought. But if emotion and cognition are inextricably linked then it is important to harness emotions and use them in your favour rather than allow them to operate against you. This is where identifying how you feel at various points in time becomes important. If emotions are influenced by everyday events and how we interpret them, they are also coloured by moods. The way in which you feel about an event will be coloured by the mood in which you find yourself at that moment. Moods can change rapidly, and indeed, it is not always possible to explain a sudden shift in mood.

Where emotions are varied, moods fall into one of two categories: positive or negative, *ie* good moods or bad moods. Performing while in a positive mood invariably provides enjoyable, challenging competitive racing. In contrast, a negative mood is reflected in irritability, dissatisfaction and ultimately in a 'bad day at the office'.

Positive moods are also thought to influence the brain's biochemistry. Part of the brain contains a system of nerves that act as a 'reward pathway'. In short, this means that the brain seeks the next 'hit' in a manner akin to addiction. Let me start here with an evolutionary example. The act of sexual intercourse at the point of orgasm provides an intense physiological pleasure that 'rewards' the brain for its activities. Having experienced it for the first time, we set out to seek it time and time again. We crave the reward previously experienced. Any experience that provides a great deal of pleasure can act in the same way. Arguably competitive racing provides a similar element of intense physiological pleasure; we race because of the addictive 'hit' it provides. So mood affects performance both psychologically and physiologically. It is how you interpret, or misinterpret, these physiological signals that can influence your racing positively or negatively. Although it is quite acceptable to go in search of this physiological reward, it is important to bear in mind that racers need to remain objective about the information they are assessing. If you lose sight of the wider picture it is easy to misinterpret information. This chapter together with chapters 8 to 12 will help to highlight the signals and symptoms you need to look out for.

So, physiology plays an important role in the way information is interpreted by the 'racing brain'. You will be familiar with stress from your own experiences. There will have been days when everything seemed to go wrong. Technical faults, suspension problems, gearing ... the list goes on. How you dealt with those problems psychologically dictated how you performed during the race weekend.

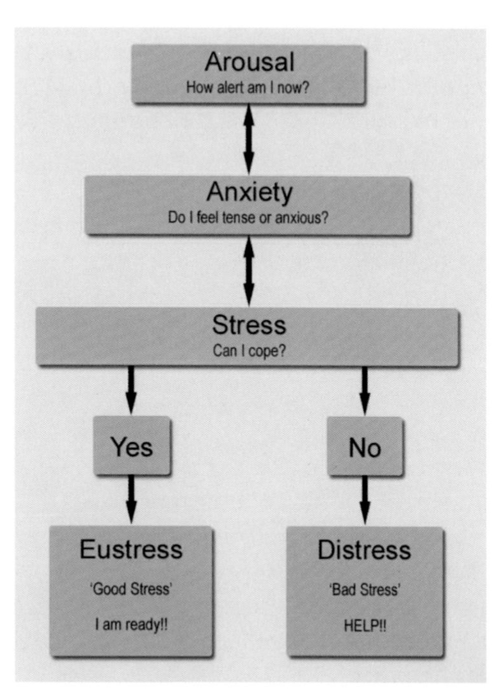

The relationship between arousal, anxiety and stress. (Boot-Handford)

Were you overly aggressive on track? Did you lack the feel and finesse usually present in your racing? Were you preoccupied with trivial occurrences that played on your mind? Did you feel under more pressure than normal? Any of these things could have been present because you were unable to cope with the situation, or because you interpreted your own feelings of physiological arousal incorrectly. If you did, then you put yourself into a position of stress.

In order to define the term stress, it is necessary to put things into perspective by going back two steps, to bring in the concepts of arousal and anxiety. As the diagram below shows, stress is the overall process of interpreting the body's state of arousal in an anxious or non-anxious manner.

I shall consider each of these elements in turn, in order to build up a picture of how the situation escalates to a point where stress becomes too much and performance drops as a consequence.

Arousal

Arousal can be thought of as both a physiological and a psychological state. Even as you read this chapter you are inevitably experiencing a state of physiological arousal, even though your heart rate is perhaps nestling around 70 beats per minute, your pupils are no more dilated than normal, your breathing is slow and relaxed and your body is in a state of balance or equilibrium. Psychologically, you are perhaps motivated to read on, processing the information on this page successfully. Alternatively, you might have just finished the previous chapter and are beginning to lose concentration. Your mind is perhaps in need of a break before you return.

Optimal levels of arousal contribute to successful performances. (LAT)

If we consider a performer's physiological arousal before a race weekend, the story differs completely. As race day beckons, I would expect your state of physiological arousal to change. I would like to think that your arousal increases to an optimal level so that you are physiologically ready to perform when you are on the grid, in the same way that your engine is at optimal temperature for the beginning of the race.

Again, it is possible to explain this state in evolutionary terms. The human body possesses a defence mechanism that responds to danger, the so-called 'fight-or-flight' response that we examined in Chapter 2. Of course, since there is now little chance of being eaten by predators one might think that this response mechanism is no longer necessary, but this is not the case. The fight-or-flight response still protects us from the modern-day equivalents of predators. If you trip as you are walking down a set of stairs, your heart rate will increase immediately, providing oxygenated blood to the muscles, your pupils will dilate and you will automatically put out a hand to grab the rail. You are responding to the danger in order to protect yourself from harm. There is no element of cognition involved. It merely happens. Similarly, as you fly through Craner Curves on a motorcycle, there is one section of track that is likely to spit you off if you get it wrong. If this happens, the fight-or-flight response kicks in automatically to prepare you for the danger, but by this time is too late and the accident has already happened. This is because, in evolutionary terms, the human body was not expected to be travelling at speeds in excess of 20mph. However, the response remains pre-programmed.

Hans Selye developed a conceptual model to explain a person's physiological response to stressful situations of this type. The model comprises three stages: alarm reaction; resistance; and exhaustion. The alarm reaction is another term for fight-or-flight. This is the immediate, short-term response to a stressful emergency situation. If the stressful situation occurs over a longer period, the human body goes into endurance mode and begins to resist or cope with the demands. In terms of racing, this could be similar to the racer who, having led a championship for the first half of a season, is under pressure to retain it for the remainder. If they fail to maintain their position in the championship table, it may be that coping with the situation has depleted the body's resources and the racer is now exhausted in the physiological sense of the word. The human body will invariably become depleted of fuel in the same way that an engine exhausts its supply of petrol. Both need refuelling at appropriate moments. I will discuss this in more detail later in this chapter, when I talk about stress from a psychological perspective.

Early psychologists saw the relationship between arousal and performance as linear, *ie* the higher the arousal, the better the performance. This sounds appealing and seems to confirm the idea of getting psyched up for the race. This 'drive theory' can be seen in the figure below.

It seems, therefore, that a simple solution to the arousal issue would be to find out what that optimal level of arousal is, so that you can gear up to that

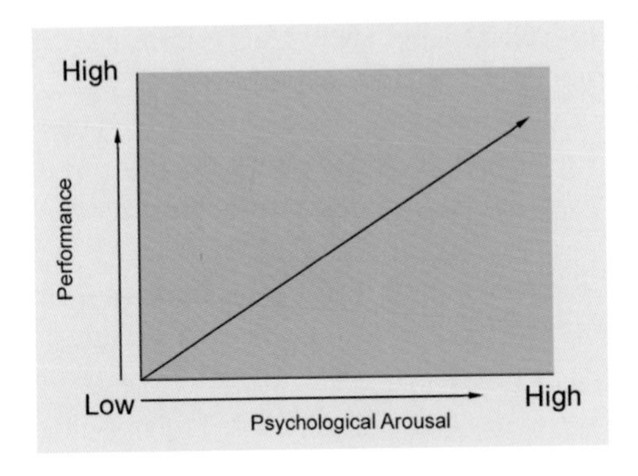

The 'drive theory': performance–arousal relationship. (Boot-Handford/Author)

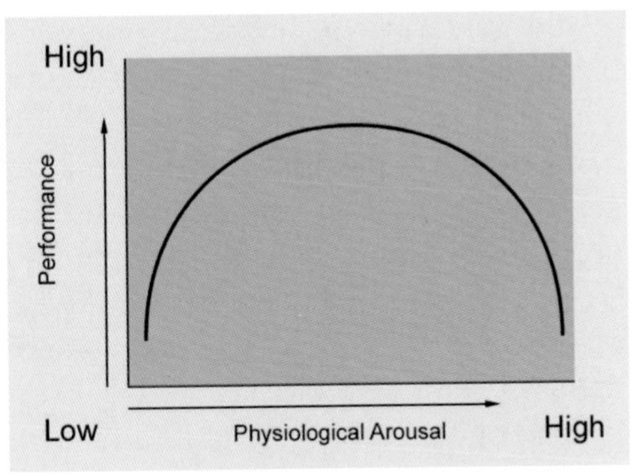

The 'inverted-U hypothesis': performance–arousal relationship. (Boot-Handford/Author)

heightened state. Not quite! It may be the case that your arousal level has built up so much over the course of the race weekend that it is too high and may, in fact, be detrimental to your performance. In this instance you would need to reduce your arousal to optimal levels. This leads us nicely on to what theorists call the 'inverted-U hypothesis'. Put simply, and illustrated in the figure above, this proposes that performance improves as arousal levels increase to an optimal level. If this optimal level is exceeded, performance begins to take a drop and suffers.

Neither theory fully explains what is happening when situations suddenly deteriorate. This is where the so-called 'Catastrophe Theory' offers us some idea of what may be happening in our heads. Hardy and Fazey (1987) suggest that increased physiological arousal is okay as long as cognitive anxiety remains low. For you, this means that if your thought processes start spiralling out of control, you are more likely to experience a 'catastrophic' event; you will do something wrong and perhaps very silly! On the other hand, if your physiological arousal is high but you are in control of your thought processes then it will be business as usual.

A basic measure of physiological arousal can be obtained using heart rate monitors, such as those developed by Polar. The equipment comprises a chest strap transmitter and a wristwatch-type receiver. The transmitter picks up the heart's electrical activity and sends it to the receiver for storage. Some of the more advanced monitors enable the data to be downloaded onto a PC via an infrared connection. This is useful in displaying the heart rate data as a waveform on a computer screen for easier interpretation, as shown in Chapter 2. It would not be difficult to map this onto telemetry data.

With practice the transmitter can be worn under a race suit and not be noticed by the person wearing it. This is important, since an ill-fitting chest strap or one that the wearer is unused to may act as a distractor and take focus away from important issues of racing. I usually ask racers to wear the equipment for sessions in the gym, on the treadmill or exercise bicycle, to get used to the feel before taking it onto the circuit even for test days and practice sessions, let alone a race.

On its own, a physiological measure such as this is insufficient to help competitors. It is the interpretation of the data that is of importance. It is here that psychological aspects of arousal start to become significant. If you are aware that your heart rate is too high, or indeed too low, you must ask the question, 'Why?' What events led to that situation, what was your perception of those events, and was that perception appropriate for the circumstances? It is at this point that I need to return to the inverted-U hypothesis, which is widely accepted in sport psychology among performers and trainers. Although it appears to offer us answers to the arousal–performance relationship, it does not, however, address these vital psychological factors that play a role in how we perform. In order to take this line of discussion further I shall introduce the concept of anxiety here and go on to discuss two of its sub-types: somatic anxiety and cognitive anxiety.

Anxiety

I would anticipate that every person who picks up this book will have experienced anxiety in some form or another. We all feel anxious at times during our daily lives. This anxiety may, and usually does, manifest itself when we compete. But do we really know what anxiety is? Do we know how to identify which type of anxiety we may be suffering from, or whether we are in serious trouble, suffering from both types? Do we know how to control our anxiety when necessary? I suspect not. This section addresses these questions. I will begin by exploring the idea that individuals may be predisposed to anxiety (a character trait), while it may also manifest itself with a forthcoming situation (a specific state). I will then deal with somatic and cognitive anxiety.

Trait anxiety is a predisposition towards anxiety. Perhaps you are an anxious person in many situations. If this is the case, you might say that this is one of your many traits, or characteristics, that make up who you are. In terms of racing, it could mean that you would experience a high level of anxiety towards a race because it is in your nature to do so. In contrast, state anxiety is a reaction towards a specific event. You are not usually anxious at any of the circuits, but today, at this circuit, you are suddenly feeling really anxious.

Although both these types of anxiety would appear, and indeed can be, damaging, the role of a sport psychologist is to help competitors identify whether they are trait-anxious individuals or whether they suffer from competitive state anxiety. It then becomes possible to put interventions in place to overcome any difficulties that these may be causing. Amongst other things I would discuss with a racer is how they feel about their pre-competition nerves. If trait anxiety is established to be an area of concern, the sport psychologist and competitor will attempt to work through underlying sources of the anxiety, changing the way in which these sources are thought about. The chapter on cognitive restructuring and self-talk is useful in helping to remedy the situation. Do not think for a moment that if you are identified as being a highly trait-anxious person, that the situation is irredeemable!

Both trait anxiety and state anxiety can be measured by questionnaires, used in conjunction with interview and discussion. A common state anxiety questionnaire in use at present is the Competitive State Anxiety Inventory –2, which measures both somatic and cognitive anxiety, as well as confidence, and looks at the present – the here and now of the competition – rather than the generalised view of anxiety that exists with the trait approach. The sample questions below are derived from the *Competitive State Anxiety Inventory – 2* (Martens, Burton, Vealey, Bump and Smith, 1990) and the *Sport Competition Anxiety Test* (Martens, 1977). They are used for illustrative purposes to provide you with an idea of the kind of questions you should ask yourself before a race.

Self-test questions derived from CSAI-2 (State Anxiety)

1. Am I feeling nervous?
2. Am I experiencing self-doubt?
3. Does my stomach feel 'knotted'?
4. Am I concerned about choking under pressure?
5. Am I feeling 'jittery'?
6. Am I concerned that I might not do as well in this race as I could do?
7. Am I concerned about a DNF?

If your answer to the questions above is 'yes', Chapters 8–11 will help you to reduce pre-race anxiety.

8. Is my body feeling tense?
9. Am I feeling ready?
10. Does my body feel relaxed?
11. Am I feeling 'comfortable'?
12. Am I feeling self-confident?
13. Am I feeling at ease?
14. Do I feel that I can meet the challenge?

If your answer to questions 8–14 is 'yes', you appear not to have any pre-race anxiety. Well done! If it is 'no', Chapters 8–11 will help you to reduce pre-race anxiety.

Self-test questions derived from Sport Competition Anxiety Test (Trait Anxiety)
These questions relate to your competitiveness in all aspects of your life, not just in racing.

1 Do I feel uneasy before I compete?
2 Do I worry about making mistakes when I compete?
3 Do I worry about not performing well before I compete?
4 Do I feel 'queasy' before I compete?

If your answer to the questions above is 'yes', Chapter 10 will help you to change the way you think about your trait anxiety.

5 Do I find competing against others socially enjoyable?
6 Am I calm before I compete?
7 Is setting goals important to me when competing?
8 Do I enjoy competing in activities that require considerable amounts of physical energy?
9 Am I a good sportsman/woman when I compete?
10 Do I notice my heart start 'racing' just before competing?

If your answer to questions 5–9 is 'yes', you appear not to experience trait anxiety. If it is 'no', Chapter 10 will help you to change the way you think about your trait anxiety and this may change with a little work from you. Question 10 is dependent on HOW you view an increase in heart rate. If you view it as a way of providing you with a rich supply of oxygenated blood to the muscles, this is a good thing. If you view it as 'un-nerving', it is contributing to your anxiety and needs to be changed.

If we accept that you are not high in trait anxiety, I would then direct attention to the specific event. In order to explore pre-competitive state anxiety I need to examine somatic and cognitive anxiety in greater depth. The word 'somatic' means 'of the body'. Symptoms of somatic anxiety are therefore physical and related to the body. The table below lists some of the more common elements, or symptoms, of somatic anxiety. Look through the list and tick those that you have experienced before a competitive event.

Symptom	**Tick if applicable**
Increased perspiration	
Clammy, sweaty hands	
Dryness in the mouth	
Increased need to urinate	
'Butterflies' in the stomach	
Increased heart rate	
Nausea	
Muscle tension	
Physical tiredness	
Irritability	

If you experience these types of symptoms before competitive events, the next question I would have is, 'At what point do you experience them – minutes before the lights go out, an hour before, a day before, a week before etc?' In establishing when the symptoms emerge, it becomes possible for the sport psychologist to introduce relaxation techniques to help eradicate these symptoms. It also allows him or her to explore the reasons underlying their emergence. It is convenient now to explore cognitive anxiety, which may be responsible for producing some of these physical symptoms.

Cognitive anxiety is basically worry. It is that portion of anxiety that is influenced by thought processes. Thought processes are used to appraise various situations that you may find yourself in. A negative appraisal of these situations is the precursor to cognitive anxiety and may, in extreme situations, lead to the phenomenon known as 'choking' or 'freezing'. This can be inferred in situations such as sitting on the starting grid, knowing that you need a good start to protect your position in the championship standings, and then experiencing a sudden panic when the lights go out and you seemingly freeze, unable to co-ordinate the clutch and throttle or accelerator to make a smooth start. In addition, worry about future events or situations and their outcomes or consequences is an element of cognitive anxiety (Lavallee et al, 2004). This implies that fear of failure and worry about what people might think of your performance are important determinants of anxiety. I would strive to help competitors restructure the way in which they appraise important situations. This is covered in more detail in Chapter 10.

The message is, however, very clear. Anxiety can be debilitating. It can get in the way of routines, strategy and rational thought processes, and can upset the psychological balance necessary for calm, clinical performance. This is what we mean when we say that we are experiencing stress. As illustrated earlier in this chapter, it is a state of what Selye (1983) called 'distress'.

Ironically, anxiety can also be facilitating, and Selye coined the term 'eustress' for this effect – shorthand for 'euphoric stress', where the body is in a positive state because of the way the stress is being interpreted. As such, then, the word 'stress' becomes redundant in the term 'euphoric stress', and for the purpose of clarity I would prefer to use the expression 'euphoric readiness', thus removing any connotations of negative terminology. When I call this a facilitative state, I mean that the positive spin placed on how you are thinking about your race is working for you rather than against you. You are happy that the thought processes are working as efficiently as your engine is. Using this analogy, in some cases your engine may not be running at 100 per cent efficiency or may be showing signs of giving up the ghost. If this is the case, cognitive anxiety is likely to be debilitating if you expect to keep racing at full pace. If you accept that the engine is under-performing, you can keep cognitive anxiety under control by asking yourself what it is that you need to do to keep circulating lap after lap to nurse the car or bike home. Your goal becomes one of scoring points, which will stand

Sudden, inexplicable actions may have catastrophic consequences.
(David.WillowPhotography.co.uk)

you in better stead than employing an all-or-nothing strategy and probably coming away with nothing. Your perception of the challenge is, therefore, vital in controlling the level of cognitive anxiety that you experience. If you lose it in your head, your body will tense up, this information will feed back into your head, and you will interpret it in a negative way. A vicious spiral then emerges and a so-called 'catastrophe' will ensue. Indeed, as I mentioned earlier, the term 'catastrophe' has been used by sport psychologists to explain sudden drops in performance that seem to come out of the blue.

Hardy and Fazey argue that if cognitive anxiety is relatively high and arousal levels are low, performance will be optimal. If, however, cognitive anxiety is relatively high and arousal levels are also high, performance will suffer considerably. For racing, the key is to identify a level of arousal at which you feel comfortable to perform. You can do this by using the heart rate monitor mentioned earlier. You should then focus on the kind of thoughts that run through your mind before and during the race or session and identify whether they are acceptable or not (whether they are positive or negative). If there are any negative thoughts, replace them through cognitive restructuring. Finally, combine the positive thought processes with your preferred level of arousal and you have a recipe for success! The table below summarises this for you:

Step 1	Identify the demand placed upon you.
Step 2	Identify your perception of that demand.
Step 3	Ascertain your psychological and physiological response to that perception.
Step 4	Replace inappropriate thoughts where necessary.
Step 5	Observe/reflect/record your behaviour in response to the situation.

Of course, it is very easy for me to sit here and provide a recipe for success, but when things are not going well it is easy to lose sight of the way towards a solution. In the next section I will cover the negative aspects of stress in more detail, before going on to explain ways of identifying and coping with it.

Where do your stresses come from?

Stress comes from either personal or situational sources. The list below shows a variety of life experiences that may cause you stress. Look through the list and tick any items that you have experienced during the last three months. The more you have ticked, the more prone to stress you may be. Don't expect to race successfully unless you can evaluate and rationalise these stressors.

	Recent life experiences
1	Disliking your daily activities.
2	Disliking your work.
3	Ethnic or racial conflict.
4	Conflicts with in-laws or boyfriend's/girlfriend's family.
5	Being let down or disappointed by friends.
6	Conflicts with supervisor(s) at work.
7	Social rejection.
8	Too many things to do at once.
9	Being taken for granted.
10	Financial conflicts with family members.
11	Having your trust betrayed by a friend.
12	Having your contributions overlooked.
13	Struggling to meet your own standards of performance and accomplishment
14	Being taken advantage of.
15	Not enough leisure time.
16	Cash flow difficulties.
17	A lot of responsibilities.
18	Dissatisfaction with work.
19	Decisions about intimate relationship(s).
20	Not enough time to meet your obligations.
21	Financial burdens.

22 Lower evaluation of your work than you think you deserve.
23 Experiencing high levels of noise.
24 Lower evaluation of your work than you hoped for.
25 Conflicts with family member(s).
26 Finding your work too demanding.
27 Conflicts with friend(s).
28 Trying to secure loans.
29 Getting ripped off or cheated in the purchase of goods.
30 Unwanted interruptions of your work.
31 Social isolation.
32 Being ignored.
33 Dissatisfaction with your physical appearance.
34 Unsatisfactory housing conditions.
35 Finding work uninteresting.
36 Failing to get money you expected.
37 Gossip about someone you care about.
38 Dissatisfaction with your physical fitness.
39 Gossip about yourself.
40 Difficulty dealing with modern technology (*eg* computers).
41 Hard work to look after and maintain home.

The survey of life experiences: A decontaminated hassles scale for adults, (Kohn ad Macdonald, 1992).

The importance of an event and the role of uncertainty within that event are common sources of stress amongst performers. Event-importance is a key factor in raising stress levels. Yet event-importance is only a label. If you do not allow yourself to be sucked into the hype and, instead, treat the event as just like any other, then you will minimise its importance, thus enabling you to concentrate on the process of racing when your competitors are focusing on the 'what if I fail?' scenario common in racing, and, indeed, other sports. A good example of this can be seen in the way Lewis Hamilton followed his win in the 2007 Canadian Grand Prix with a win in the US Grand Prix at Indianapolis seven days later. Expectations were high, but stress was minimised.

The uncertainty of a situation may undoubtedly have an adverse effect on your racing, but only if you are not in control of environmental factors. The key, therefore, is to establish the greatest degree of control you can. This might mean discussing appropriate issues with anyone, from the team manager to the person who looks after your helmet, to ensure that everything that can possibly be done in support of your focus is being done.

I discussed self-esteem in relation to confidence in Chapter 4, but the lower one's self-esteem is – which is based on the perception of one's ability – the

Exercise as much control as you can under the circumstances. (LAT)

higher anxiety is likely to be. The consequence is a potential dip in performance, or the failure to reach one's potential in the first place.

It is widely accepted amongst sport psychologists that what is important here is the need to consider how personal factors interact with environmental factors to produce or to minimise stress. Remember, stress is in your head. It is only real if you let it become real. By changing the way in which you think about these factors, you are exerting control over the situation. Racers should be well versed in psychological skills training (PST), such as imagery, self-talk and goal setting, in order to cope with stress and anxiety. There is no reason to believe that this should be any different in motorsport. The PST chapters in this book provide the keys to unlocking your potential to control anxiety as you choose.

What should you do now?

If you are experiencing stress, three simple avenues to explore are hydration, diet and fitness. Any imbalance between these factors may be contributing to stress. Fatigue, dehydration and poor fitness (or over-training) may be affecting your concentration, focus, reaction times and many other aspects of your racing. These are covered in the next chapter.

Chapter 6

Nutrition and hydration, exercise and fitness

"It is good practice to seek help from experts outside of one's own field." In producing this chapter, I have enlisted support from my colleague, Annie Lambeth, from the University of Worcester. Annie is an expert in Sports Nutrition, providing guidance to athletes both through our Human Performance Laboratory and through our Sport Performance and Coaching Centre. Her advice is the basis for the guidance provided in this chapter.

COMPETITORS MAY BE TEMPTED to grab a quick bite to eat on the run, or want a quick fix of a burger, hot dog or bacon roll from a trackside fast-food stand in order to keep them going. Food and water tend to be given lower priority during race weekends, though it must be remembered that they are the body's 'fuel'. You would not dream of going out on track with insufficient fuel or water in your car or bike, so why should your body be any different?

The first part of this chapter will discuss the importance of adequate hydration or fluid intake. If you are dehydrated, your brain will not function optimally and you will probably have a headache – the simple urine chart provided overleaf will assist your assessment of adequate hydration levels. The second part of the chapter will provide advice to help you eat appropriate, nutritionally balanced foods, which will help you prepare for and get through race weekends. In the final part we go on to discuss how exercise and physical fitness influence performance. It is pleasing to know that racers at the higher levels of achievement see the benefits of exercise and fitness programmes as a means of enhancing their endurance and stamina for racing. Fitness training is an excellent way of preparing for forthcoming races. Nevertheless, there are dangers associated with such regimes, especially if the drive to reach peak fitness reaches extremes and exhaustion sets in just as race day appears. This chapter provides guidance on all these issues.

Hydration

Hydration is easy to overlook and can cause problems at crucial moments. Dehydration does not affect you immediately, but if allowed to develop it will affect all aspects of your performance, and may do so at the most inappropriate of times. To put this into perspective, if the human body becomes dehydrated by as little as 2 per cent, physical performance can be impaired by anything up to 20 per cent. If dehydration levels increase further muscular strength is reduced and perception of effort is increased, which significantly increases fatigue. This is how serious and important fluid intake is. In addition to these physical effects dehydration directly impairs brain function, which slows down the decision-making processes, reduces skill and accuracy, is detrimental to attention, and reduces concentration. At 160mph, such problems are not good!

Added to the fact that you may not have paid enough attention to how much you have consumed, once you are kitted out in your racing suit, boots, gloves and helmet, sweating is going to do little to help improve your hydration level. This is

Adequate hydration is vital for successful brain function. (Aston Martin Racing)

Dehydration is more likely to occur when the temperature rises. (LAT)

'Brolly dollies' do more than simply look good. (Author)

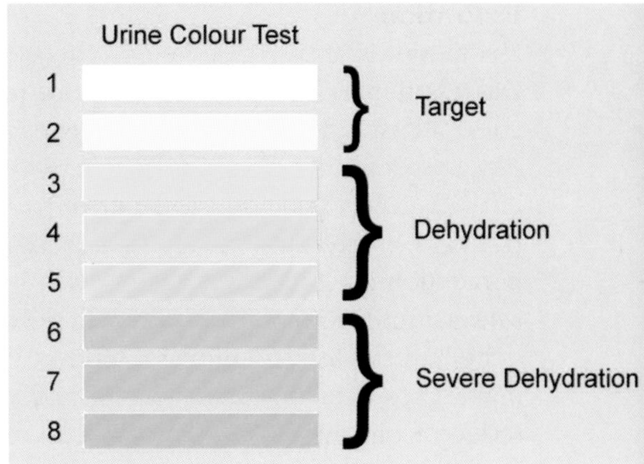

Urine colour test. (Boot-Handford/Author)

especially the case during the summer months, or during international race days where the climate is hotter than competitors are used to or have had sufficient time to acclimatise to.

In such circumstances, I would suggest that you pay particular attention to fluid intake, and make sure that you drink as much as possible, even if you do not feel thirsty. Alternatively, the responsibility of keeping your 'tank' full could be entrusted to a member of your team personnel.

It is usual in motorcycle racing for 'brolly dollies' to be on the grid before a race. While their role in this corporate environment might be to provide 'eye-candy' for male members of the public, teams, sponsors and the like, they also serve a far more important role. In my view, brolly dollies are essential in protecting racers from exposure to excessive heat on the starting grid. As track temperatures coincide with increased heat from race wear, which in turn coincides with increased heat from the numerous engines at the starting line, the grid is an unpleasant place to be for too long. Yet racers can be on the grid for more than five minutes in some cases, and in this time can begin to overheat. The brolly dolly can protect you from the damaging effects of exposure to the sun, and this is far more important than splashing the corporate logo around the grid. A cool racer is an effective racer. Keep the corporate identity for the hospitality tent afterwards.

The easiest way to monitor hydration levels is by keeping a check on urine colour. The chart above gives an idea of varying urine samples and their link with hydration levels. The general rule is, the darker and more cloudy the colour and the stronger the odour, the more dehydrated you are. In checking this, I would assume that a racer has adopted balanced nutritional eating habits. It is important to be aware that vitamin tablets colour urine quite considerably because the kidneys do not absorb all of the vitamins. It is also important, therefore, to ensure that checks are done beforehand if you take daily vitamin tablets. The same can be said for taking caffeinated energy drinks. As some racers show a preference for drinks such as Red Bull, this piece of information is important, since it renders the urine chart useless. If this is the case you should keep a log of fluid intake instead. Just as technicians keep full records of engine mapping and suspension settings etc, where possible you should keep a full record of how these drinks affect you physically, physiologically, nutritionally and psychologically. If you have a successful day or a day where nothing seems to go right, then you can reflect on these records to see where it went right or wrong.

Nutrition and hydration records can serve a vital role for the following season when correlated with performance data. Take responsibility for your own optimal levels of functioning. It might reduce your lap times by a second or two! Indeed, I would advocate that all team personnel should take responsibility for their own hydration and nutrition requirements. Fluid and food intake directly influences brain functioning. Arguably, therefore, all team members with important and perhaps stressful roles should benefit from optimising their own level of functioning.

Replacing fluid loss is vital to your performance. (Rimstock plc)

I should draw attention to another area of hydration that is not always considered important or even considered at all: post-race re-hydration. It is just as important to ensure that people re-hydrate themselves, wherever possible during racing. Your typical heart rate will increase to around 180 beats per minute during a race. This is equivalent to a highly demanding sprint in running. Of course, to spectators the impression is that 'all' a racer has to do is sit in a car or on a bike and race. If these spectators saw exactly how much exertion the heart was being subjected to they would be amazed. The hidden elements of physical exertion are sometimes overlooked when racers are preparing for the next race or for the forthcoming season, although I am pleased to say that sports science is playing a far greater role nowadays than a few decades ago. Racers are now deemed to be athletes in the true sense of the word. Once you understand the need for adequate hydration, nutrition and fitness, you will be able to concentrate so much easier, your decisions will be sharper, and racing will be so much more pleasurable.

Always ensure that you have re-hydrated after a session on track – check that your urine looks clear. Another quick way to check your hydration is to weigh yourself. Hop on the scales before and after each day's sessions. For each kilogram of body weight lost you need to consume 1½ litres of fluid.

One final comment about fluid intake is that a drink with some sugar and sodium in it (check the nutritional information) will be absorbed into the body faster than plain water. Most sports drinks are specially designed to be the optimal concentration for absorption, but make sure you like the flavour – if you don't like the taste you are less likely to sip it, and risk becoming dehydrated.

Nutrition

If you are feeling lethargic during the days leading up to a race, one of the things it makes sense to explore is your eating routine. You may be forgiven for thinking that the role of nutrition is to provide energy-promotion, but this is not necessarily the case. There are no magical meals that can be eaten to guarantee success. But there *are* foods that are more or less appropriate for a sports-person.

I have known racers who raise their blood glucose levels by eating sweet foods or taking soft drinks, which are notoriously high in sugar. This might appear to be the ideal solution – a quick burst of short-term energy to last the session – but although it will indeed raise blood glucose levels for a while, there is also an associated side effect, the 'crash', in which those levels nosedive, usually to a point lower than they were to start with. This so-called 'rebound' effect will potentially happen 30–60 minutes after consuming a high sugar drink or snack. The resultant low blood glucose level and associated drop in concentration, energy and focus is not something you want to occur in the middle of a race. Consequently, I would not advocate such 'quick-fix' snacks, but instead recommend slow-release, slower digested foods such as muesli bars, cereal bars, low fat sandwiches and bananas.

When to eat?

In evolutionary terms, the human body was not designed to interpret incoming sensory information at anything faster than running pace. It was necessary to look out for animals that were likely to eat us; the faster we could spot them and the faster we could run the better! The autonomic nervous system is responsible for the way in which we respond to this type of 'threat' and is known as the fight-or-flight response, as discussed in chapters 2 and 5. When we are strapped into a car, ready to go out on track, this evolutionary response is still present (although we can minimise it with practice) and it is responsible for various processes (*eg* dry mouth, butterflies in the stomach, the need to urinate, sweaty palms etc).

In a fight-or-flight situation, one important process that temporarily ceases is that of digestion. This is because all available energy resources are taken up with dealing with the threat. Digestion is not a survival-promoting activity when urgent action is required. Consequently, if you have eaten a heavy or inappropriate meal before going out on track, your stomach is acting as nothing more than a huge carrier bag, which may give you indigestion or stomach cramps – both of which will undoubtedly influence mental functioning. Therefore it is a good idea to eat a

Choosing the most appropriate food is an important and often overlooked element of racing. (Aston Martin Racing)

Maintain your fitness levels and vary your training sessions throughout the year. (RenaultF1)

meal two to three hours before heading onto the track, to allow your body time to digest it. This needs to be slow digesting food so that you are neither hungry nor suffer from a sugar 'rebound' during the race. Foods such as pasta, rice, sandwiches, jacket potatoes and cereal are ideal.

What to eat?

The first thing that needs to be pointed out is that there is no single set menu that you should adhere to. Obviously, people have different preferences and tastes. So this section will simply provide guidelines that you can adapt to suit your own needs and special dietary requirements.

You can start the process a few days before a race weekend, when you should consider eating fish and chicken rather than red meat, and pasta or rice meals rather then fried foods or takeaways. When having pasta dishes, try to go for vegetable-based sauces rather than cheesy ones, which are high in hidden fats. Snack on low fat biscuits, cereal bars, bananas, fruit and nuts to avoid hunger between meals. Avoid tempting snacks such as pastries, cakes and chocolates in the days before a race, and on the day of the race itself, so that you can maximise your intake of energy-rich foods without taking in too much fat.

Don't start the day off with a large fried breakfast, as it will sit heavily on your stomach. If you must have a large fried breakfast, you should at the very least ensure that you do so as early as possible. Try to go for grilled bacon or sausage and poached or scrambled eggs rather than fried. For lunch, avoid burgers and chips and go for pasta dishes or something with vegetables. For snacks, you should take bananas, nuts and oatmeal biscuits such as Nairn's Rough Organic Oatcakes. These will all help to reduce hunger, which can really interfere with your concentration.

Exercise and fitness

The general rule of thumb is that overall physical fitness, acquired through appropriate and regular exercise regimes, is undoubtedly of benefit to all. If you have the luxury of being able to schedule exercise programmes in a fitness suite three, four or perhaps more times a week throughout the year, this is an excellent way of keeping fit if you are embarking on a season of races. During the winter break you will be able to continue with your schedules, and take holidays to help relax, unwind and re-energise yourself. In combination with exercise programmes, the ability to relax will help in preparation for the new season. So, we have a difference between physical fitness during off-season periods and physical fitness throughout the season. Nevertheless, generally speaking, the greater your level of fitness, the more control you will have over your performance.

Off-season fitness planning

There is no real danger of over-training during the off-season. This period allows plenty of time for exertion and recovery and, consequently, is perhaps the best time for you to push yourself to the limits of mental and physical endurance. Such practices are aimed at building stamina and mental toughness, the psychological elements of which are discussed in Chapter 12. Planning a fitness programme depends primarily on available resources and demands made upon your time. I know racers who complement their fitness suite work with moto-crossing, snow-boarding, skiing or sailing. Equally, there are racers who prefer to stay within the environment of the fitness suite. So, while time demands and available resources will play important roles in your choice of fitness programme, the key to its success, arguably, lies in choosing something that provides an element of pleasure whilst also being beneficial to your style and level of racing. By doing this, the likelihood is that you will remain motivated to continue training, and it is this motivation that helps spur people on when times are tough, cold or wet, or when something less strenuous seems infinitely more appealing.

I once worked with a racer who ran a lap of the circuit the night before a qualifying session. He had also been training during the five or six days beforehand and was recovering from a frenetic race weekend seven days earlier. He crashed during qualifying, and after much deliberation admitted privately that his error was caused by exhaustion. As a learning experience this was excellent, in that he now understands the symptoms he needs to watch out for under such circumstances. Before this he lacked sufficient knowledge to interpret these symptoms effectively, but nowadays he never goes into a race weekend physically over-exerted.

Race fitness

Race day is the culmination of all the preparations for competition. Equipment, technical data, tyre and suspension information all come together to form a coherent package for the race. It should be no different for you, the racer. Through exercise and fitness your nutrition, hydration and energy levels should be at their optimum. I would advise racers not to participate in any exercise that is remotely strenuous on race day. By all means walk or jog around the circuit on the evenings leading up to the race, but on race day itself your energy resources should be reserved for racing and nothing else. Light exercise is permissible if its

Fitness levels contribute to recovery from injury. (sutton-images.com)

Even a short micro-nap can be beneficial to performance. (sutton-images.com)

purpose is psychological, *ie* if it is being used to reduce tension or anxiety, to psyche yourself up, or to induce a positive mood. Alternatively you might do some light exercise to loosen up physically. There should be no other reasons for its use on race day.

Sport psychologists generally agree that exercise and mood are linked. The brain's reward system, discussed in Chapter 7, seems to be activated as a result of exercise. Put simply, if you are feeling low, the evidence suggests that you will feel so much better after a period of exercise. What better way go into a race weekend than on a high? It is the feel-good factor that rewards us.

Rehabilitation following injury

A physically fit racer is also preparing him- or herself for the after-effects of that inevitable crash that is always just around the corner (pardon the metaphorical pun). In the event of a crash and the resulting damage it may do to your body, a high level of physical fitness will help in the rehabilitation process.

Obviously, no one would advocate you crashing in order to test this, and indeed, it is hoped that the guidance offered in this book will help in minimising the risk. Nevertheless, crashes are inevitable aspects of motorsport, and with this in mind psychonutrition is as important in recovery and rehabilitation as it is in enhancing performance. Essentially, a physically fit body that receives appropriate nutrition and hydration is best suited to assist in the rehabilitation and recovery process.

What next?

You probably have a whole host of questions now. When should you train? How much should you train? When should you stop? When should you step down a gear? How do you time it to peak on race day? Of course, the answer to all these questions will be different for all of us. There is no single piece of guidance on fitness regimes. My advice, beyond this chapter, would be to have a fitness assessment and organise a session with a personal trainer. There are many books available on fitness training, and it is not my intention to provide specific guidance on fitness regimes here. The references at the end of this chapter will give you some guidance. The authors have worked with athletes from many different disciplines, providing bespoke consultancy services through the Sport Performance and Coaching Centre at the University of Worcester over several years (www.worcester.ac.uk/spcc). Alternatively a simple web search will provide services closer to home. The key is to ensure that you receive quality provision from experts within Sport Science as it relates to motorsport.

A word on sleep

A final issue to consider is how much sleep you should have before a race. If you have organised a night out on the evening before a race, cancel it! Don't assume that you can get by on a few hours of sleep and expect to get out on track and perform successfully, or indeed safely; you may even still be over the alcohol limit. Apart from the obvious dangers of alcohol, it will also severely dehydrate you, and the effects of dehydration were discussed earlier.

As a precautionary measure, you should consult your GP before embarking on any changes to your existing dietary and fitness habits. The information in this chapter is for guidance only.

Chapter 7

The brain's reward system

Introduction

It may seem rather odd to be reading about brain physiology and biochemistry in a practical text on psychology in motorsport, but all will be revealed as you read on. In Chapter 3, I suggested that racers may receive a physiological 'hit' rather like an addictive reward for successful performances. I went on to link this to the human drive to seek out pleasurable rewards again and again. I suggested that the resulting physiological change in brain chemistry is, by its very nature, a highly motivating experience and is one that helps to maintain motivational levels. So, the easy answer is for racers to compete simply to satisfy addictive cravings. Well, not exactly. To adopt this view would be simplistic in the extreme. Instead, this chapter provides guidance that will allow you to understand how your brain functions during competition, how brain function influences performance, how addictive competitive motorsport can be, and how an understanding of this addiction is important in this high octane world.

I begin by exploring the two evolutionary divisions of the brain that are important for motorsport, and go on to discuss the brain's 'reward' system and the role of addiction. Finally, I outline the role played by the sensory systems, which are responsible for providing the brain with the perceptual information upon which a racer must act. Though I accept that many readers may wish to switch to 'more relevant' chapters, I would urge you to persevere and read on. I will endeavour to keep explanations at an accessible level and believe that you will be fascinated by how your brain functions.

The brain: hemispheres

The brain can be divided in many different ways, but the most common distinction is between left and right sides, or hemispheres. At a very general level these do not process identical information; instead, certain aspects of brain function are associated with one or other hemisphere. The left hemisphere deals largely with analytical and language abilities, and is the hemisphere that evaluates information, forms strategies and verbalises expletives as you lose the back end coming out of Copse Corner. In contrast, the right hemisphere is the one that appreciates art, music and all things creative. However, it is also dominant in synthesising elements together into a whole. You might evaluate and analyse all aspects of a GP circuit, noting bumps, adverse cambers etc with your left hemisphere, but it is your right hemisphere that is responsible for appreciating the grace, beauty and finesse with which you negotiate that circuit. When working together, which is an undeniable event, the two hemispheres provide all the information you require for success at any circuit. The only time this fails is when your internal demons cast doubt on the information your brain is processing. But that must be left to another chapter.

The evolving brain

As well as viewing the brain in terms of left and right, or, to use the correct term, laterality, it is possible to view it in terms of layers. To help you visualise this, consider the rings of a tree. The brain does not comprise rings, but it does have three distinct layers. Way back in our evolutionary heritage, the paleomammalian, or reptilian, brain emerged. This is the innermost region of the brain. It is the bulbous end of the spinal cord inside the skull and is responsible for all survival functions, such as respiration. If this area gets damaged, you will not be alive to notice. This is arguably the reason why it is protected so deep inside the skull. Next comes the mammalian brain. This is the middle region of the brain and is responsible for irrational, emotional functions. Finally, the outermost region of the brain is the cortex, responsible for our cognitive thought processes. As the brain has evolved, it has grown not only in size but also in complexity. Its folds and undulations allow more surface area to be crammed into a small space, in the same way that if you fold an A4 sheet of paper four times it will occupy a much smaller area but can still hold a great deal of information. The brain's evolution has also resulted in new functions being added. This is a type of refining process. Once the basic survival mechanisms were present, the next layer (emotion) could be added, and then the final, rational layer. Think of how race technology has improved and you will begin to see some similarities.

The cortex: the rational brain

If you think of the bark of a tree as being at its outermost part, then it is easy to remember that the cortex is the outermost part of the brain. Of course, one difference is that the brain is encased inside the skull and is covered by the scalp and hair, all of which help to protect it. Another difference is that trees are unable to think!

As we have seen, the cortex is the newest region of the brain in evolutionary terms. It is the rational part, responsible for thought processes or cognitions. As

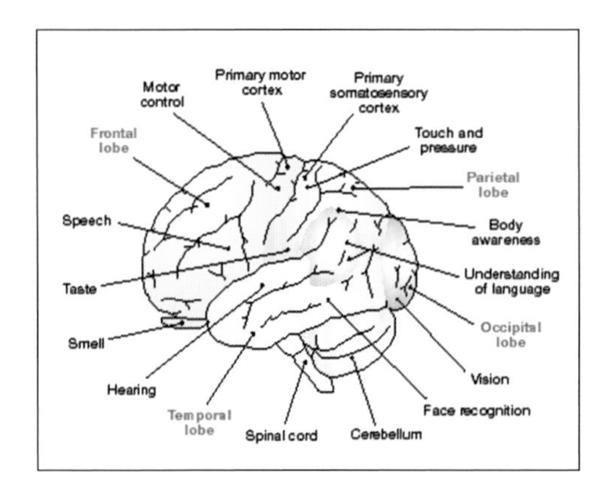

Illustration of the human brain: hemispheres and cortex. (Matthew Marke)

with the hemispheres, the left and right parts of the cortex control thought. The left part is also responsible for producing speech and for comprehending the speech of others. It is the cortex that enables racers to communicate their needs clearly and effectively, and team personnel to understand and interpret this information appropriately. Any behaviour that is influenced by emotions is receiving input from an older brain region, one that needs to satisfy basic urges. The key to successful motorsport performance lies in the interpretation of these urges by the cortex. The practical chapters on goal setting, self-talk and cognitive restructuring will assist racers in interpreting such non-rational information in a rational manner.

The sub-cortex: the irrational brain – the hypothalamus and the 'four Fs'

The hypothalamus is a region of the brain beneath the outer layer of the cortex. It is part of the sub-cortex and nestles firmly in the irrational section of the brain. As I take pleasure in explaining to my students, the hypothalamus helps to control the so-called four Fs: fighting, fleeing, feeding and procreation. It usually takes a few seconds for the penny to drop, but I use the phrase because my students seem to remember the four functions more easily that way.

In evolutionary terms, fighting and fleeing is the 'fight-or-flight' response to danger discussed in earlier chapters. It is the body's way of preparing us for one or other response. The hypothalamus is also responsible for providing our drive to eat and procreate, two more evolutionary necessities that promote our survival.

In motorsport terms the hypothalamus is partly responsible for the reaction experienced when an opponent suddenly appears from nowhere, disappears up the inside and pulls away. It is also responsible for the sudden panic experienced when you realise that you are exiting the track as a result of a forced error or sudden mechanical breakdown. Consequently, it is at the very moment when you need your rational brain to resettle your physiological and psychological states that it is overpowered by signals from the irrational brain. However, the information in this book will provide the tools you need to get you back to business quickly and efficiently, rather than letting a situation escalate into an ever-increasing spiral of despair and frustration.

The amygdala and aggression

The amygdala is a structure within the brain's limbic system, or emotional system. It is an area of the brain that influences aggressive behaviour. As was the case with the hypothalamus, the amygdala is responsible for diverting a racer's attention away from the task in hand. Consider how you felt the last time an opponent did something that you considered dangerous or irresponsible, or attempted to psyche you out. You may have reacted perfectly rationally. However, you may also have reacted with anger or frustrated aggression. If you manage to stay on the circuit the consequence of this reaction is that you have fallen into your opponent's trap and are now playing to their strategy rather than your own.

Frustration may escalate into aggression if left unchecked. (LAT)

Moreover, you are probably acting irrationally and this seems to fuel your feelings of aggression towards your opponent. This leads to you focusing your attention on them rather than on your own strategies and goals, and you become distracted and pre-occupied with beating them.

I have seen the effect of this time and time again. If you watch televised racing you will often see two racers competing to 'outdo' each other in this way, only to find that the racer behind them has been lying patiently in wait and pounces at the most opportune moment. If I had £1 for every time I have heard of racer X losing two places as a result of his or her racetrack battle against racer Y, I would be considerably richer than I am!

The brain's fuel system

It is all very well my explaining which brain regions have an effect on performance when there is, of course, nothing you can do to improve them unless you are a qualified neurosurgeon. The key lies in identifying the symptoms associated with different types of behaviour and addressing them. Brain regions, however, are only part of the story. Brain activity is a combined process of electrical and chemical activity.

The brain's chemical system is an area you need to be aware of since it is one that you may be able to influence. This is what I mean by the brain's 'fuel system'. The brain contains a set of different chemical substances called neurotransmitters, or nerve-impulse transmitters. Once created, these are responsible for ensuring that nerve signals jump across tiny junctions between nerves and make temporary connections with the next set of nerves. The illustration below shows a neurotransmitter crossing the gap between two nerve cells, enabling the brain's message to continue on its journey. Dopamine leaves nerve number 1 and locks onto sites at nerve number 2 once it has travelled across the gap.

Neurons in the brain send electrical signals to each other and connect via a chemical called a neurotransmitter. (Matthew Marke)

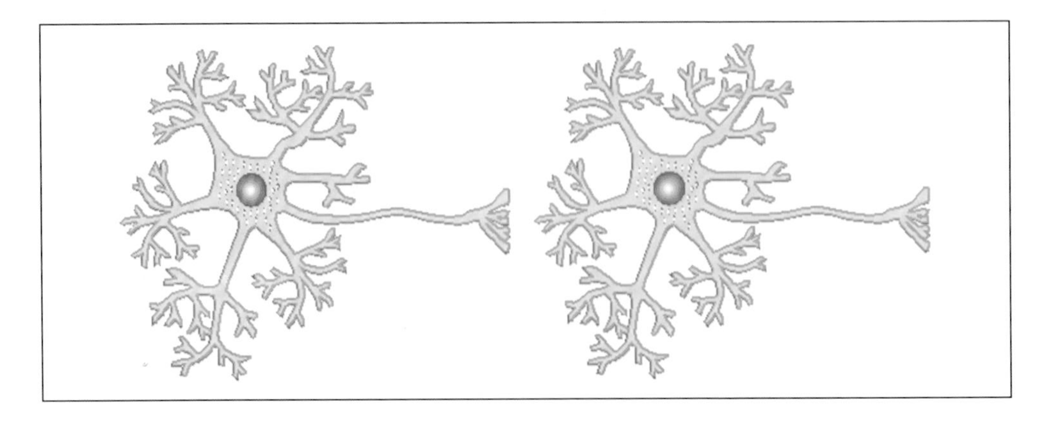

Different substances are responsible for different functions and will affect performance. The table below provides some basic information on these substances and their functions.

Some common neurotransmitters and their functions	
Dopamine (DA)	Related to addiction and its control; movement; learning; and attention.
Norepinephrine (NE)	Related to control of wakefulness and alertness.
Serotonin (5-HT)	Related to control of sleep and arousal; aggressive behaviour; eating behaviour; regulation of pain; depression.
Acetylcholine (Ach)	Related to control of skeletal muscles.

Are racers addicted to winning? (LAT)

The dopamine pathway

It is the dopamine pathway that interests me in motorsport. To give it its technical term, it is known as the meso-cortico-limbic dopamine system. While this sounds incredibly complicated, it simply means that the pathway runs through areas of both the rational brain and the irrational brain. It is the pathway that is responsible for reward or addiction. A shot of dopamine tells the irrational section of the brain that the person feels good, *ie* it provides a reward for whichever activity caused it to happen. This information is then interpreted in light of the situation and the rational part of the brain conveys the perceived reasons for this feel-good factor. The person then seeks out this feel-good sensation again and again.

Although I am using the term 'addiction' to describe this state, I do not intend you to think this is a bad thing. Of course, there is much in the way of negative press surrounding addiction, usually addiction to drugs. Nevertheless, by definition the need to win and the associated reward received by the brain is indeed an addiction. However, this is an addiction to chemicals produced naturally by the

BELOW: *The brain's chemical reward provides an emotional 'feel-good' factor.* (LAT)

RIGHT: *A lack of chemical reward results in an emotional 'feel-bad' factor.* (David.WillowPhotography.co.uk)

Arai
MJK
CHAPMAN
CHAPMAN
MJK
MJK

human body. The only time this addiction takes on negative connotations is when striving to acquire the hit becomes obsessive and begins to impinge on other aspects of daily functioning.

The schematic diagram below provides a usable flow chart to illustrate the reward process in a practical way. This clearly shows that the situation contributes to a change in brain chemistry, which stimulates brain regions to create a change in emotional state. A feedback loop is responsible for feeding back in to review the environmental situation.

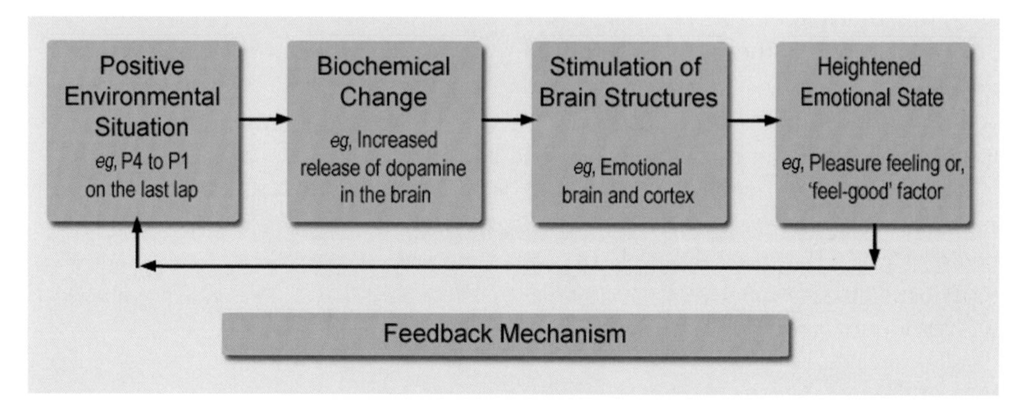

Of course, the system can be applied in negative situations, where reward is not obtained. This is evident in the diagram below, which shows that dropping back from first place to fourth in a race will not elicit the release of additional dopamine required, and this will manifest itself in a negative emotional state, the 'feel-bad' factor.

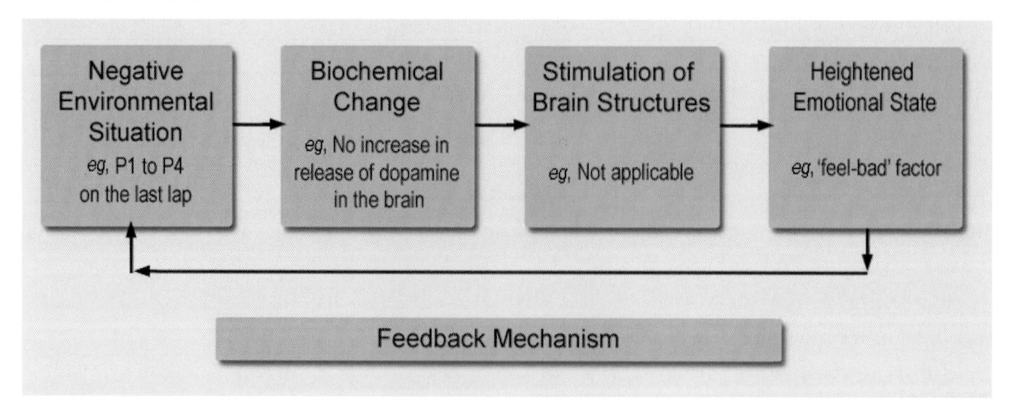

Having outlined the process by which the brain receives its reward and how this relates to emotional, mood and motivational states, it is now necessary to consider two opposing theories regarding why humans seek out this reward. One, known as the physical dependence theory, suggests that humans obtain the rewarding sensations (or feel-good factor) from the experience and become physically dependent on those sensations. In this way we are forced to seek out the sensations in order to satisfy our cravings. If we do not obtain the reward, we experience symptoms of withdrawal.

In contrast, the hedonistic-incentive (or pleasure-seeking) theory is far easier to live with, and this is the one I favour. Put simply, it suggests that humans tend to be hedonistic by nature and that incentives are attached to pleasurable experiences, in terms of the rewarding, feel-good factor. So we tend to go in search of pleasure-seeking activities, such as motorsport, to obtain our hit. Indeed, even the anticipation of that reward is sufficient to cause the brain to release extra dopamine. Such is the power of addiction. So, as you move up from fourth place to first you anticipate staying in front and winning the race. Your brain rewards you in anticipation of the outcome and this fuels your motivation to keep the throttle pinned to get the job done.

As a racer you can subscribe to either of these theories to explain why you compete. Having this knowledge will not help you to win races or even to race better. However, knowing how the reward system can affect your emotional, mood and motivational states will help you to identify the symptoms associated with 'good' or 'bad' performances.

Perceiving environmental information

In this chapter I have discussed the importance of interpreting or perceiving incoming information in positive ways to get the most desirable result. Indeed, that is the message throughout this book. It seems that it is not the sensory information coming into the brain that is important, but rather the quality of a racer's interpretation or perception of that information.

Perception is linked to action in one of two proposed ways. One, known as the information processing theory, holds that information comes into the brain for analysis and comparison with previous knowledge and experience, rather like a computer. Following analysis a decision is made regarding which response to make, and then the action takes place. So, if you see a gap open up on the left of the racing line, you compare the information that your eyes are providing with stored knowledge, such as where you will be positioned for the following corner if you take the line where the gap is at this corner. Memory will then help you decide whether to carry out the manoeuvre. The information processing theory holds that we perceive, and then we act.

This is all well and good. However, the problem lies in the fact that the human brain evolved to function at nothing more than running pace, as humans were unable to go any faster. As a result, in the example just described the brain has insufficient time to react to the situation, since it was not built to travel at speeds in excess of 15–20mph. Those people who favour this theory would simply argue that experts in motorsport are well versed in their skills and react quicker as a result of learning. I would tend to support the theory for many aspects of daily life. However, in terms of motorsport an alternative theory exists, referred to as direct perception, which explains perception and action in a more successful way by arguing that they occur simultaneously and we become 'tuned in' to the correct information in our environment. Let me explain using the motorsport example above. Environmental information comes into the brain to be dealt with and acted upon immediately. No previous knowledge and experience is required and no decision is made regarding which response to make. So, if you see a gap open up on the left of the racing line you immediately 'see' the gap and nothing else. You do not consider the relative distance of the racers who are on the periphery of that gap, it is just there for you to exploit. Information regarding positioning for the following corner will become available as soon as that information conveys itself to your eyes. Memory is not important because the situation is never the same twice. You will never be at exactly the same place on the track, at exactly the same speed, with exactly the same opponents doing exactly the same thing as on the previous lap. On high-speed sections of the track you do not decide whether to carry out this manoeuvre, it just happens. The direct perception theory does not contend that perception must come before action, but that perception and action are inextricably linked.

Of course, at this moment I would not be surprised if you were somewhat sceptical. 'A racer doesn't need memory, decision-making ability or experience? Yeah, right.' But this is the beauty of the direct perception theory. Though I would agree that knowledge and experience are undoubtedly vital elements of successful racing, I would also remind you of your early days in racing when you were, or indeed still are, learning your craft. Thinking, decision-making and storing information in your memory provides the knowledge you need to race and, yes, it no doubt helps during a race, but there are days and situations when thinking too much is detrimental to your performance. Perhaps it was responsible for your not reaching a state of 'flow' on the track when it really mattered. This is when the direct perception theory becomes appealing. It suggests that you do not need to think but simply to act, almost intuitively. All the information is waiting for you to tune into it, and in the ever-changing racing environment in which you become immersed direct perception provides the key to success.

A subtle flaw in this theory is that if all the information is in the environment and enters the brain for direct action, how can we ever get things wrong? The answer is simple: by being attuned to the wrong information. This is somewhat similar to tuning in to the correct frequency on a radio: you only need to be 1MHz off-station and you will receive nothing better than loud crackles and hisses. But tune in properly and all becomes crystal clear.

Arguably, using direct perception should prevent racers from being affected by distractions. If a racer is tuned in correctly distractions are still present but are outside of the frequency range. Decisions cannot be influenced by emotions, stress or anxiety because they are not part of the perceptual process. Of course, whether this is actually the case or not is speculative. You might argue that this would be

When an opportunity appears you have already started to take it, almost without thinking. It just seems to come naturally. (Caterham Cars)

similar to putting the radio in an area of poor reception and expecting it to perform well. Indeed, there is no answer to the debate about whether one theory is better than the other. The point I wish to make here is that direct perception may be more applicable to racers who have learned their craft and are in need of tools to hone and refine it. By adopting a different perspective when considering incoming perceptual information, performance may improve dramatically. I cannot tell you how to perceive directly. It doesn't work like that. The key lies in how you think about situations and events that happen. If I forget what I want to say while giving a lecture to 200 students, I immediately perceive it as a minor blip in concentration and I move on as if nothing has happened. If I thought too much about the situation it would have a detrimental impact on my performance. Similarly, and I say this elsewhere in the book, if you spend too much time thinking about the last corner that didn't go well you will mess up the next three corners too, and probably the next lap into the bargain. Instead you need to try tuning in to slightly different aspects of the environmental information next time around and test it out.

It is important to obtain a healthy balance between racing and daily life. (ASA/LAT)

Concluding remarks

Having provided you with an insight into the processes that take place in your brain, I do not intend for you to go away believing that you are an addict. This is not my point. My intention is that you should understand your need to race, to win and to be the best. Being addicted to success is no bad thing as long as it does not interfere with happiness, relationships, family and other things in your life.

However, being addicted to rewards can adversely influence your racing unless you know how it is affecting your brain, which is the reason for including this chapter. The information I have provided on the way that nerves in the brain function will help you to understand what is happening when you feel tired, lethargic or depressed, as well as energised, strong or ready to do battle with the world. It is the way in which you interpret these feelings that is important. If you get the interpretation wrong, your whole race or race weekend may be affected.

Having explored the possible pitfalls to success in competitive motorsport, you are now ready to acquire the tools you need to deal with them. The following chapters provide practical guidance on how to deal with challenging situations.

Chapter 8

Goal setting

SETTING GOALS is an ideal way of progressing in motorsport. Consider such people as Jenson Button and Lewis Hamilton, who began their careers in karting and have now progressed to the upper echelons of motorsport. Similarly, the motorcycling legend Valentino Rossi began his racing career on 125cc bikes before moving up to meet and beat the challenge of Moto GP. So, is goal setting the key to success? No! *Achieving* those goals is the key to success. In my own experience, competitors commonly set themselves goals that are either unrealistic, overly vague or are too distant and subsequently become demotivating. (I will discuss motivational issues later in this chapter.) Examples of such goals include,

Outcome goals are not helpful to progress. (Volkswagen UK)

respectively: 'I want to beat the existing lap record by five seconds'; 'I just want to do well this weekend'; and 'I want to drive in Formula 1 in 12 years' time' (well OK, the obvious exception here might be a certain Mr Hamilton). Personally, I have set myself two goals for this chapter. My first is to explain why unrealistic, overly vague or distant goals are unhelpful for competitors; and my second is to explain how to set appropriate goals using a technique known as SMART.

What is goal setting?

Goal setting can be considered in a variety of ways. For example, it focuses on setting targets based on reaching a certain level of proficiency. Setting appropriate, specific goals helps to improve performance and enables levels of motivation in achieving these goals to continue. Essentially, it is target setting.

Which perspective: outcome, performance or process goals?

Sport psychologists suggest that there are three different types of goal. It is important that you are aware of the differences between them:

Outcome goals

As you might expect, outcome goals are based on the end product of a performance: on its outcome. By the very nature of outcome goals, the frame of reference is a comparison between your own performance and that of your opponents. How many times have you checked your lap times against those of your opponents when the timing sheets have been released? You are comparing yourself on outcomes. In sport and, indeed, in many aspects of business, outcome goals are prevalent. It is not my performance that is important, rather it is whether I, or my team, brings home the trophy. So, 'I want to win the race' is an outcome goal. A competitor who has come last, yet who has just ridden or driven the ride/drive of his or her career has failed to achieve the set goal. Not only is this demotivating but it also does not take into account any success other than that controlled by other people. As I explain to my clients, this kind of goal setting cannot be of any benefit whatsoever. Of course, it is quite acceptable for other members of the race team to think in terms of outcome goals for a competitor. The key is to ensure that *you* do not enter the race with outcome goals.

In an ideal world, however, I would attempt to convert team personnel to the same way of thinking, to avoid conflict. One only needs to look to World and National level championships midway through the calendar to see high-profile race teams dispensing with the services of 'under-achieving' racers.

Performance goals

Performance goals may be seen as diluted versions of outcome goals. In essence, they are related to a competitor's performance regardless of the outcome. An

Goal setting is about setting targets. (sutton-images.com)

example of a performance goal might be to achieve consistency of lap times within a time window of 1:18.00 to 1:17.25 minutes/seconds at a particular circuit. I would argue that performance goals are preferable to outcome goals, since they relate directly to a competitor's development. A good reason for setting such goals is in order to modify an existing performance goal to see if you can push the envelope that little bit further.

Process goals

Arguably the most appropriate kind of goal setting involves examining the process of competing, the 'flow' required to get the bike or car around the circuit swiftly and smoothly. Process goals are, therefore, about 'how it feels'. Think of a time during your racing career when everything went so well on the circuit that you could have stayed there all day and not put a foot wrong. You hit every apex, every line was spot on, gear selection and throttle action were sublime. I would ask you to recall a race like this when setting goals for the forthcoming race. So your goals would be set on the basis of doing the job rather than on the end product or outcome.

I worked with a racer who put his right knee out on the approach to Druids at Brands Hatch, long before his opponents did. It transpired that he was doing this as a way of setting up the bike before putting his knee down again at the appropriate moment to tip the bike into the turn. His process goal was to find a way of setting up for the turn so that he could go through at a speed that he felt was appropriate for him. Every time he approached Druids he was faster than his opponents (outcome) but was only interested in 'getting it right' (process).

For every corner at every circuit, it should be possible to set a process goal that enables you to get the most out of your racing experience whilst at the same time expanding it. You can do this by working out what information you will need to perform the process successfully. For example, you may counter-steer, put your knee down, shift your weight or use the heel-and-toe technique to gain maximum entry and exit speeds. The key is to strive for the correct feel, and to take this knowledge into the race: 'I missed the apex on the last lap because I didn't counter-steer. I have another nine laps in this race to practise this.'

Is setting process goals the simple solution?

Although the idea of setting process goals might seem convincing, the simple answer to this question is, 'No.' Competitors may enhance their performance by employing a combination of goal-setting strategies, but such a tactic would be ill advised until they are sufficiently familiar with the goal-setting technique. As is the case with acquiring physical racing ability and expertise, mental techniques require investment of time and effort before they can be adapted to suit changing situations.

How does goal setting work?

Knowledge of how goal setting may exert its effect on performance in general will help you to understand how to set effective goals and how goal setting can be utilised in directing your attention; channelling effort; improving stamina; and developing new strategies of learning how to overcome challenges. Let us examine each of these in turn:

Performance goals relate directly to how you have done out on track. (sutton-images.com)

Directing or focusing attention

It is important to direct attention towards a specific goal. Competitors who do not focus on specific goals usually find themselves floundering and their attention easily distracted from racing. This might include not paying adequate attention to the feel when coming onto the start-finish straight after the last corner. If attention is directed at getting drive out of the corner at the earliest moment, the competitor can focus on this as a goal. Essentially, the competitor is breaking down the overall task of racing into small, manageable chunks that can be developed during free practice and qualifying sessions; a sort of, 'I need to do X and Y if I want to do Z' approach.

Channelling effort

Having focused your attention on a specific goal, as in the example above, you then need to make a concerted effort to achieve that goal. On its own, therefore, directing attention is not enough. Active effort is also required in achieving the goal. You need to evaluate how you are going to achieve it.

Improving stamina

Having directed attention and mobilised effort in pursuit of the goal, the next step in the process is persistence. In attempting to achieve the goal, it is of no benefit for a competitor to direct attention and mobilise effort for only the first few corners of every lap. It is not enough to persist for the first five laps of a 25-lap race. Persistence means having the stamina to keep going for the duration of the session or race.

Competitors who appear to get stronger as the race progresses show signs of persistence. It is the endurance element of racing that provides a 'never give up' attitude. Goal setting helps competitors to pick opponents off as the race develops, or to get the most out of qualifying sessions. Consider the frenetic activity during final minutes of qualifying. Who is in pole position? Who is on a quick lap? When should I go back out to steal pole and prevent anyone else from having the time to take it from me? We only have to look at elite level motorsport at any race weekend to see this unfold. Persistence is one of the keys to unlocking success in this activity. I will return to the issue of stamina in Chapter 12.

Developing new strategies of learning to overcome challenges

Having directed attention, mobilised effort and persisted in the activity, you are finally able to develop new strategies of learning. This ensures that you do not become stale and demonstrates adaptation to the ever-changing circumstances. Think of this as being similar to evolution. No species remains the same. Instead it adapts constantly to the changing environment. A competitor on the circuit should be striving to adapt to different situations, taking opportunities when they emerge and looking for the most appropriate strategy for each situation. So, if you went through Church, at Thruxton, the fastest corner of any British circuit, at 115mph, your new goal might be to go through at 118mph next lap, 120mph on the following lap and so on, until you have reached either the limit of adhesion, as dictated by the laws of physics, or the limit of your own ability. If you reach the limit of your own current ability, then your goal should reflect the fact that it is possible to go through the corner faster and your role is to explore the boundaries of your ability. Under these circumstances, it becomes necessary to learn new strategies for overcoming the reasons for your slow speed through the corner.

Whether you achieve your goals may also depend on the following:

Ability

I have hinted at ability above. Your ability is an obvious point in considering whether you can actually complete the task successfully. There is no point in saying that the 2004 British Superbike Champion John Reynolds can go through Church at speeds in excess of 130mph if you simply do not possess sufficient skill to do the same. However, you might strive towards a goal approximating to it, yet within the realms of achievability for yourself. As you develop as a racer, who knows where your goal for this corner might take you?

Commitment

It is vital for a competitor to be committed to achieving the goals that he or she has set. If commitment is absent, there is very little chance that the goals will be achieved, at least in part because the desire must also be missing. A few years ago I saw a rider go back to the motorhome during free-practice because it was raining. He did not really feel like riding in the rain. This may have been based on a commonsense assessment of the weather conditions and safety issues. Arguably, however, it also shows a lack of commitment. Had I been working with this rider, I would perhaps have established some 'wet weather' goals for the session, after asking the question, 'What will you do if it rains on race day?'

Feedback

Feedback is a vital element of goal setting. Feedback provides the competitor with a way of evaluating whether the goal has been achieved or not. Of course, there are objective measurements that are of use in establishing whether a goal has been achieved, such as lap times, sector times, telemetry data etc. I would argue that subjective information is also relevant in terms of feedback, but only if it can be quantified. For example, I might ask you to rate the feel of a particular corner on a scale of 1–10, where 1 is poor and 10 is excellent.

So, 'How did Clearways feel on a scale of 1–10 on the last five laps?' Let's imagine the answer is 3, and of course, this is unique to that particular competitor

Providing feedback is an essential element of effective goal setting. (LAT)

on that particular occasion. I would then ask you to explore ways in which you might approach and go quicker or smoother through the corner, and ask you to go back out in the practice session and strive to improve on the 3 rating. You would explore this by altering the braking point, turn-in, or how early you get on the power on the exit of the corner. Although this is subjective, it does offer a way in which performance can be measured. If it links with telemetry or other data, then it should provide supporting evidence to the competitor.

Task complexity

The complexity of a task may influence its effectiveness as a goal. Setting a particular goal of achieving a lap time in the wet that is too close to a dry lap time would be fruitless on the grounds that the task is more than likely too complex. It is important, therefore, when setting goals that they are realistic, given the complexity of the task. Similarly, if a competitor has recently moved up to a higher level of motorsport it would, perhaps, be inadvisable for him or her to set goals that seasoned contenders at that level would strive to achieve. I always advise competitors who have made the move up to establish goals that would be appropriate for a learning period. As a result I do not get disconcerted by what others perceive as 'poor' results, on the basis that their opinions may be based on outcome goals, when the competitor is successfully achieving process goals. Again, this goes back to my earlier point about setting achievable goals to provide confidence, retain motivation and ensure that development is taking place. Of course, there are always exceptions, notably Lewis Hamilton during the 2007 F1 season. Nevertheless, Hamilton's goal-setting strategy will have been based on similar principles.

The setting of inappropriate, outcome goals can lead to problems with self-confidence, anxiety and satisfaction. The more confident you are, the greater the likelihood of achieving the goal. Sport psychologists call this 'self-fulfilling prophecy'. If you believe that you will fail, you *will* fail. If you are confident that you will achieve, then you will. Additionally, each performance has a certain amount of anticipated satisfaction attached to it. When goals are achieved, satisfaction increases, confidence grows and motivation to achieve the next goal remains strong.

Regardless of the theoretical perspective one adopts, goal setting remains one of the most important techniques in sport psychology in helping competitors to develop skills and achieve success. The effective use of goal setting is imperative in this development, and it is to this that I turn next.

Effective use of goal setting

From my experience with elite level competitors, it is apparent that a lack of appreciation and understanding of goal setting has led performers to set inappropriate goals, or to think about their performances in the wrong way. When asking performers what their goals are for a forthcoming competition, I frequently hear such statements as, 'I want to win,' or, 'I want a podium this weekend.' In itself, this is all very well. However, the difficulty lies in the fact that you are unable to control everybody else on the grid. The immediate response is usually, 'Well, I will simply get to the front of the pack, lead from the front and then stay there to the chequered flag.' Brilliant! But everyone else is probably thinking the same thing. By approaching goal setting from a different viewpoint a podium position or first place is not as important as the process of achieving successful personal growth through the race. Once a competitor understands this, their performance should improve and the podium will beckon as a side-effect or consequence of the process. Telling competitors not to focus on winning is amongst the hardest things I have to do in sport psychology. But improving your performance through setting appropriate goals is like putting money into a savings account: at some point in the future it will provide you with everything you need. However, it is far easier to persuade younger competitors of this, since they are

Focus on achieving your process goals, not on winning the race. (sutton-images.com)

more responsive to taking new ideas on board. Perhaps this gives anecdotal support to the old adage 'you can't teach an old dog new tricks'. Of course, I do not agree with this adage; but it makes my job of convincing older competitors of the benefits of appropriate goal setting more challenging.

If I ask racers who they consider to be the best person on the track, the answer is very rarely, 'I am.' But I say to them: 'In fact, you *are* the best person on the track – but perhaps not at this very moment, for reasons that we need to investigate and resolve. So go out and beat the best person – yourself; improve and refine your skills, achieve your goals, and leave the result for someone else to be concerned with.' If you set out to improve on existing skills you are less inclined to get sucked into an opponent's strategy, will develop as a driver or rider, and are more likely to end up on the podium.

How does goal setting apply to motorsport?

Goal setting applies to motorsport in the same way that it applies to performers in any other sport. As a racer, I expect that you already possess a comprehensive knowledge of what is required to carry out the tasks at hand. You are aware of how a race weekend unfolds. You are aware that importance is assigned to different things on different days – for example, selecting the right gearing is perhaps less important during free practice than achieving the most appropriate suspension setting. Of course, by race day you would expect to meet both your requirements. Goals should be set, therefore, to suit the individual requirements of each session, in addition to having goals for the whole weekend.

Guidelines for writing your own goals

Various goal-setting systems exist in sport psychology. However, most involve three logical, progressive stages: preparation and planning; education and acquisition; and implementation and review or follow-up.

Preparation and planning

It is important for you to assess your abilities and needs. For me, a competitor's input is essential and will guide me in my assessment. A useful method of keeping motivation levels high is to set wide-ranging goals, so that a competitor can work on different elements at different times. I may, for example, help you to set goals related to physical fitness when you are not competing. It is important to plan to help achieve the strategies you have put in place, so that you are aware of whether progress is being made. For example, we may agree to use goal setting to:

- Aim for a specific race in the championship.
- Overcome motivational or confidence problems.
- Aid the development of physical fitness, racing technique and/or mental preparation for competition.

- Identify and plan common goals for your team.
- Help you through a programme of injury-rehabilitation.
- Assist you in recovering from staleness or burnout after a long, arduous season.

Plan and prioritise your goals by making a list. Pick no more than three goals to work on first.

Education and acquisition

When carrying out a goal-setting strategy, it is necessary to organise regular meetings to monitor performance in relation to the set goals. Some people advocate working on a single goal at a time. I would argue that it is more important to negotiate this personally with the competitor, since they may be in a position to work on more than one goal during a particular period. Again, the responsibility for appropriate goal setting rests on collaboration between the competitor and the sport psychologist.

After initial preparations, it becomes possible to observe and monitor progress in fitness, racing technique and overall confidence in a competitor's ability. As goal-progression or goal-achievement data is collected a picture builds up, and this may serve to motivate you to continue with the programme. If you are using goal setting as a means of returning to full fitness after injury, the setting of appropriate goals, given the nature of the injury, will help to prevent over-exertion. I would rather you finish the race in seventh place and pick up points, than over-exert yourself, causing more damage and potentially missing the following round in the championship.

Collect the evidence to see if you are meeting your goals.

Implementation and review

It is important that you identify relevant procedures for the assessment of goals. If you do not know how the procedures work, there is little chance of success. Throughout the process, the sport psychologist should provide appropriate support and encouragement wherever progress towards goal-achievement is taking place. You should set a date for the review of goals set. It is important to reflect on progress, achievement or reasons for not meeting set goals.

In setting a date, it is necessary to be mindful of the timeframe associated with different goals. Goals may be short-, mid-, or long-term. Of course, this distinction is specific to each competitor. What I consider is a mid-term goal may be a long-term goal to you. I will now outline each type of goal:

Set a review date to reassess your progress.

Long-term goals
These are your ultimate goals, the things you desire most from your motorsport. Do you want to become world champion, national champion, win five championships, or something else? Long-term goals can cover a single year of racing, or your entire motorsport career. You set the boundaries yourself and your long-term goals relate to your own perspective on time. If you wish to emulate Ayrton Senna, Valentino Rossi or Michael Schumacher, you must set your goals a long way ahead. However, this poses a problem in terms of maintaining your motivation for the duration of the goal-period.

Mid-term goals
Mid-term goals act as a way of keeping motivation levels alive. They serve as a focus point in a less distant future. How do you know whether you are progressing towards your long-term goal? You know because you have set and achieved a mid-term goal. Mid-term targets should be clear and should be set in relation to long-term goals. For example, if you have set a long-term goal linked to the end of a racing season, then your mid-term goal will perhaps be after the middle race. If, however, your long-term goal is a five-year plan, then the mid-term goal might be assessed at some point during the third year. An example of a mid-term goal during a single season might be consistently lapping within 1.2 seconds of your personal best for each circuit.

Short-term goals
Short-term goals are, again, relative to mid- and long-term goals. They serve as a focus point in the near future. You do not have to wait too long before a short-term goal can be assessed for progress. In keeping motivation levels high, short-term goals should provide manageable, regular opportunities to achieve success. Taking the example above, a short-term goal during a race weekend might be consistently lapping within 1.2 seconds of your personal best for five laps during the next qualifying session. In setting a personal target, rather than an outcome-based goal of a particular grid position, you can concentrate on your own strategy rather than being a pawn in others' games. Having achieved this short-term goal, you should then consider setting a new short-term goal for the next qualifying session, or the next ten minutes of the current session etc.

Common goal-setting problems
Without appropriate guidance it is easy to fall into the trap of failing to achieve the goals that have been set. If progress is not monitored, as I mention elsewhere, there will be an increasing likelihood of goals not being achieved. Indeed, if goals are not achieved motivation may diminish and performance be impaired as a result. Not only should goals be monitored, but they should also be revised or readjusted as necessary. If you have not achieved the goal you set,

then refocus or 'dilute' it so that it becomes achievable. It may be that the original steps toward the goal were simply too large. Keep this statement in your mind: 'If I chip away at my performance, I will get where I want to be at some point.'

It may also be that the goals you set are too general, or not measurable. If you are unable to measure achievement towards your goal, how do you know whether you have reached it or not? Similarly, if you set too many goals you may not be able to achieve all or any of them in the timescale you have set yourself. I will discuss these points in greater depth in the section on SMART.

Finally, individual differences play a role in goal-setting problems. I would not ask you to compare your fingerprint with mine and tell me which one is the best. In the same way, the goals you set for yourself should not be related to what other people are doing or can do. I would not expect you to set the same goal for a qualifying session as Hamilton or Rossi. I would, however, expect you to set a goal that might ultimately take you on the road to success – but then, my goal is not success but rather to strive towards improving your performance.

An introduction to SMART goal setting

SMART is an acronym for a technique that helps sport psychologists and competitors set appropriate goals. It stands for 'Specific, Measurable, Action-oriented, Realistic and Time-phased'. Let us look at each element in turn:

Setting specific goals

It is important when goal setting that you identify exactly what goal you wish to achieve. It is no use saying, 'I want to do well.' This is too general. Instead, you might wish to negotiate the second sector within one second of the lap record, 70 per cent of the time during a practice session. If you achieve this, you have the opportunity to readjust your goal. The same applies if you do not achieve this consistency. I would tend to favour competitors setting goals relevant to areas of the circuit where they are slower and where improvement is required. In doing so, negotiating the rest of the circuit becomes less daunting.

Setting measurable goals

Having set a specific goal, it is vital that some form of measurement is used to evaluate whether or not the goal has been attained. Using the above example, timing data should support the '70 per cent' goal. If you do not have immediate access to timing data, have a member of the team time you at the relevant part of the circuit and radio the information back to the pits. Think of a ruler. If I ask you to measure a piece of wood without using a ruler, the likelihood is that you will over- or underestimate its length. If you use a ruler, we both have an absolute measure that can be relied on. Absolute measures are not always possible in goal setting. Nevertheless, the aim is to strive towards precise, observable measurement wherever it is available. A measurable goal is therefore quantifiable and, as such, acts to tell the competitor whether it has been reached.

Setting action-oriented goals

As one might anticipate, action-oriented goals are goals that highlight something that needs to be done. An action-oriented goal is not about thinking about an activity, but rather is about taking steps that will change something. For example, if you have just received a new engine in order to achieve the goal of consistently fast laps, the action-oriented goal may be to use the session to find where the peak power comes in. There is little benefit to be gained from thinking about the power band when action will provide the answer. Alternatively, you may focus on what needs to be done to overcome your loss of corner speed, or your slow exit speed.

Setting realistic goals

If your goals are unrealistic there is little chance of achieving them; motivation may diminish and performance may become impaired. Setting a realistic goal will provide a light at the end of the tunnel, something that is within your grasp. If you need to get quicker, setting manageable goals that help you progress will assist in getting you to where you desire to be. It would be unwise, however, to set goals that are so easily reached that achieving them becomes meaningless. This highlights the importance of setting realistic yet challenging goals. If there is little by way of challenge, you are unlikely to receive satisfaction from the task. In writing this book, for instance, I set myself a goal of writing 1,000 words a day. I consider this to be realistic and challenging, without being so difficult that I cannot meet the goal. As a result, I have been successful thus far and get a sense of satisfaction every time I achieve my goal. If I set my sights beyond this word-count I may not reach the daily goal and this may lead to despondency. If, on the other hand, I set the goal at 500 words a day, I doubt if I would get any satisfaction and you would not be reading the book!

Setting time-phased goals

There is little use in setting goals without a deadline for review. This essentially is what I mean by the term 'time-phased'. A time-phased goal must be accomplished by a particular deadline, or target date. Again, if you set a deadline that is too soon the goal may not be achievable, so it is important to remain realistic about your expectations. You will find little benefit in setting a lap-record goal during free practice if you are not happy with the set-up of your car or bike. In a sense there is a time-phased deadline for the set-up itself – it must be ready by race day – so perhaps it would be wise to consider any goals in relation to how confident you are in your equipment. If it is not 100 per cent as you want it to be you might consider revising your goals for the race. Of course, it is possible that you may have different goals with different deadlines: you may have a time-phased goal linked to performance during the forthcoming qualifying session, but you might also have a time-phased goal of achieving consistency over a number of qualifying sessions this season. There is, therefore, an element of crossover with target dates.

Additional practical guidance on setting goals

The sport psychology literature provides additional practical advice for effective goal setting. Issues include setting performance and process goals; setting goals for training, practice and competition; recording goals; goal-commitment and support; and feedback. I briefly outline each of these issues below:

Setting performance and process goals

It is good practice to set both performance and process goals. It is also acceptable to set outcome goals, but these should be of secondary importance. Performance and process goals should provide you with the necessary requirements to achieve the desired outcome. You should concentrate on your own performance and the process you go through to achieve that performance. When setting goals you should therefore ensure that elements of the process of negotiating the circuit are equally important in striving for success.

Setting goals for training, practice and competition

It is quite common for competitors to set goals only for the race itself, or for the season, but I would advocate that you set goals for all aspects of life that relate to

Performance and process goals will help you to achieve your objectives. (Volkswagen UK)

your motorsport. So you should set goals for your physical fitness regime, for example. This will help you to compete when your body requires huge amounts of energy to drive the car or ride the bike. You may also set goals related to nutrition or to changing your eating habits to get the most from your body. (Nutrition is discussed in Chapter 6.) You may set goals for tyre-testing sessions, track days, free practice and qualifying. The message is to set goals in all areas leading up to the race itself. Preparation through goal setting is arguably as important as preparing your car or race bike before arriving at the circuit. Would you simply wheel the bike out of the van, or the car off the trailer without having fettled it since the last race? Consequently team personnel would also benefit from reading this chapter, on the basis that goal setting will also benefit their preparations for the next race weekend. Every member of the team should have a goal-setting strategy.

Recording goals

Recording goals is vital to progress. The racing season is long and drawn out over several months. If I ask you in September to cast your mind back to the first race of the season, could you remember every aspect of what has happened since then? Psychologists tell us that this is unlikely. I expect that team personnel will keep telemetry records, lap times, tyre information etc, but there is no reason why you should not keep similar records relating to your goals in a racing journal or personal log. What were the goals for each session? Did you achieve them? If not, why? What were the readjusted goals? Did you achieve them? And so on. It then becomes possible to look back over the season, review progress and reflect on the implications in advance of next season. Examples of ways in which to record goals can be found later in this chapter.

Goal-commitment and support

It is important that competitors subscribe to the idea of goals and their effectiveness in improving performance. The competitor must show commitment to achieve. All people associated with the team are in a position to foster that commitment by providing support for the competitor wherever possible. It is of no use whatsoever for the sport psychologist and competitor to work on a goal-setting programme, only for the team manager to override the programme and instead set unrealistic outcome goals. If all members of the team sing from the same hymn-sheet then achievement becomes far more likely.

Feedback

As I have pointed out elsewhere, feedback is a vital element in goal setting. Feedback can be obtained from many sources. Technical data can help determine where you are going well, or where improvements need to be made. Timing sheets provide objective performance data. Tyre technicians can provide feedback on the state of tyre wear and suspension technicians can provide input on suspension. *You* are responsible for providing feedback to all relevant members of the pit team in order to influence changes in settings. And the sport psychologist is responsible for evaluating progress on the goal-setting programme and providing feedback where appropriate.

Feedback is sometimes seen as criticism, but should not be. Rather it should be viewed as a means of communication that enables the team to further refine its recipe for success. It is occasionally necessary to remind team personnel of this fact.

I have included a summary information sheet below that I give to competitors during discussions on effective goal setting. I find it useful because it provides just enough information for competitors to refer to it quickly and easily during their hectic schedules.

Combining goal setting with performance data

One way in which racers can assess whether they have met their goal is to compare it with performance or telemetry data. Telemetry provides extensive information about all aspects of a racing car, and, in some cases, race bikes. When I work with competitors I try to gain access to the technician who collects telemetry data. By listening to the technician discussing sectors on the track where

Keep as many records as possible to help in evaluating your performance and progress. (LAT)

Goal-Setting: Competitors Summary Sheet

Competitors do not always know how to set goals effectively.
This may cause goals to be vague, unchallenging, misdirected and intermittent.
If your goals are too high, it is not uncommon for lack of motivation and self-confidence to creep in.

Effectively-set goals:

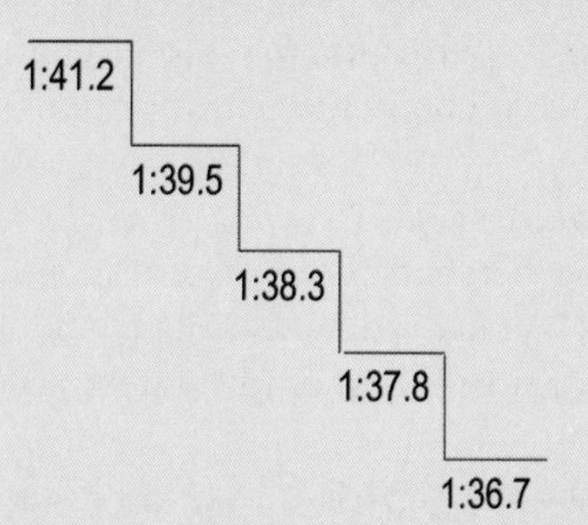

Improve performance
Improve the quality of testing/qualifying sessions
Clarify expectations
Provide a challenge in testing/qualifying sessions
Increase motivation to achieve
Increase pride, satisfaction and self-confidence

So, when setting goals, you must be SMART. Goals should be:

Specific Measurable Achievable Realistic Time-phased

Goal Setting Principles

1. Set performance or process goals, not outcome goals
2. Set challenging, not easy goals
3. Set realistic, not unrealistic goals
4. Set specific, not general goals
5. Set short-term, not long-term goals
6. Emphasise individual goals over team goals

Effectively-set goals. (Boot-Handford/Author)

the competitor is going too slowly, is in the wrong gear, or is staying on the brakes for too long, it becomes possible for me to help the competitor establish new or adapted goals. It is important to be reminded that setting outcome goals, such as securing pole, is not helpful. However, the telemetry data can provide an insight into the relationship between racer and machinery and this relationship should be exploited wherever possible.

Although telemetry is common at higher levels of motorsport, this does not always filter down to club level. Nevertheless, team personnel can provide relevant information such as timing through sectors, overall lap times and tyre or gear choices for particular circuits or conditions. Again, it is the responsibility of all team personnel to identify and make use of all available information to enhance a competitor's performance.

The next step

Having reached the end of this chapter you should now be able to set your own SMART goals. Your task now is to put these newly acquired skills into operation. The form below should be used to list your goals.

GOAL SETTING

Name: .... Date: ....

Practice or Competition ....

When setting goals, you must be SMART. Goals should be:
Specific, Measurable, Achievable, Realistic, Time-phased

Specific

Measurable

Achievable

Realistic

Time-phased

Date for review of goals:

Chapter 9

Relaxation

Introduction

It is quite common, in many walks of life, to hear the phrases 'Just relax,' 'Chill out,' 'Don't get so tense,' and variations on these themes, and one would have to agree that this is good advice for competitors in all sports. In motorsport, however, the implications of *not* being relaxed are potentially serious: a crash at 120mph or

Relaxation is an important tool in your psychological toolbox. (LAT)

more, possibly caused by tension before the start of a race, cannot be taken lightly. So my general advice would be to do just that: 'Relax.' Yet very few people are ever shown *how* to relax. It is a bit like being asked to carry out your own injection mapping to provide peak power for a particular circuit: if you do not already know how to do it, it is not possible without some form of training.

To dispel a common myth, relaxation is not simply a matter of taking a few moments to unwind, listening to some music, taking a walk and so forth. Of course, such activities can be considered relaxing, but relaxation is about so much more. Various techniques exist and I will discuss them below. Chapter 5, on emotion, anxiety and stress, also links nicely with relaxation, as does Chapter 2, on attention and concentration.

It is important to accept from the outset that relaxation training is not a simple technique that can be learnt quickly. Rather, it may take somewhat longer than competitors anticipate. The key to success is that it should be carried out in a systematic, progressive manner.

What is relaxation?

Explaining relaxation at this point would be like me telling you the ending of a new movie that you are desperate to see, or the outcome of a race that you have recorded but have not yet found time to watch. You need to experience it for yourself! Nevertheless, as the chapter unfolds it will become clear that relaxation is so much more than the state of 'relaxing'. In practical terms, relaxation is an important tool that racers can use to minimise stress in potentially stressful situations.

Sports psychologists generally agree that relaxation is a way of overcoming issues relating to over-arousal and anxiety. As I explained in Chapter 5, we all need a certain amount of anxiety in order to function properly. I am relaxed as I sit here writing this chapter, but not too relaxed. As you sit on the starting grid, waiting for the lights to go out, you should not be too relaxed, but then neither should you be too anxious. This chapter is about finding the balance, or reducing anxiety of some form or other.

How does relaxation work?

In my dealings with sports performers I have been asked the question 'How does relaxation work?' many times. My response is usually to answer with a question: 'Why do you want to relax?' What I am trying to establish here is whether the person is experiencing somatic anxiety or cognitive anxiety and requires guidance in somatic relaxation or cognitive relaxation. It is more important, at this stage, to discover their own perceptions of what they need, before I make my decision about their requirements. The same applies to you. While it gives an indicator of where to head next, you must obviously bear in mind that you may be misguided in terms of your requirements and I would explore this in more depth.

The differences between somatic and cognitive relaxation are distinct. They can be categorised as muscle-to-mind relaxation and mind-to-muscle relaxation, respectively:

Somatic or 'muscle-to-mind' relaxation

The premise underlying somatic relaxation is that the mind cannot be anxious in the absence of muscle tension. So if there is no tension in the muscles, then the messages going back into your brain must be saying that there is no need for anxiety. The key here is that you need to know what signs to look for, and I will cover these shortly when I outline four basic, yet really effective, relaxation techniques.

Cognitive or 'mind-to-muscle' relaxation

Cognitive relaxation acts in the opposite direction. Rather than the muscles providing the mind with information about tension, if the performer trains his or her mind to relax then the muscles in turn will become relaxed.

A relaxed body may reflect a relaxed mind. (Aston Martin Racing)

If you flip a coin, it *cannot* fall on both sides at the same time.
If you feel mentally or physically relaxed, you *cannot* be mentally or physically anxious.

The importance of breathing!

Each of the techniques mentioned below involves mastery of breathing. It is not enough for me simply to outline these techniques out of context. Rather, it is important to understand that appropriate breathing is a necessary requirement. This may sound strange, given that no one has ever told you how to breathe. Let's face it, you don't need instruction – breathing just happens. You have been doing it for a while now so you must be pretty good at it! It is a function of the autonomic nervous system and is controlled without thinking. If I ask you now to hold your breath for as long as possible, I will not have to ask you to stop holding your breath, it will simply happen after a short while. The type of breathing required for relaxation techniques is rather more formal and structured, yet equally simple with practice. To use an analogy, think of your body as an engine. It has a standard cylinder head with normal exhaust ports, a standard exhaust and a standard air filter. What you desire is an engine with a gas flowed cylinder head, polished exhaust ports, a competition exhaust and a high-performance air filter. When these items are fitted, then as an engine you can breathe more easily and you have unlocked extra power. This is what appropriate breathing may do for your performance.

During daily life many of us use thoracic or chest breathing. It is superficial and shallow, generally only utilising the upper section of the respiratory system. Chest breathing is fairly rapid and is associated with the rigours of daily life. In contrast, abdominal, or deep breathing is rhythmic, slow and, as expected, deep. It utilises the full capacity of the respiratory system. You can feel the difference as you read this section. Does your breathing feel shallow and irregular? Now, if I ask you to take a breath, fill your chest with air, then fill some more, and finally take one extra breath to fill your lower abdomen, you will understand the difference in capacity. When you have filled this extra space, hold your breath for the count of three and then slowly and gently release the inspired air to the count of five. Do this properly three times and I guarantee that you do will feel more relaxed than you did before starting the task. Having shown that there seems to be an immediate difference, it is now possible to practise deep breathing to feel the benefits.

Whenever you are under pressure you can use this quick and effective method of refocusing on the task to be done. So if you are on the starting grid, feeling anxious, take a few deep breaths and your tension should begin to disappear. Think of this as the sticking-plaster approach to a flesh wound. Ideally you should not be in a position on the grid where you feel unready, because your mental preparation will overcome any difficulties. However, if you need to employ emergency measures they will be at your fingertips, so to speak.

Think of your lungs as having three compartments: shallow; middle; and deep. As you breathe in, fill each section in turn *before* you exhale.

Common relaxation procedures

To recap, the distinction between somatic and cognitive relaxation should be remembered as a quick and effective way of establishing preliminary information about tension and anxiety. I will now discuss four common techniques used to elicit relaxation: progressive muscle relaxation; autogenic training; meditation; and biofeedback. I will then conclude by introducing the idea of an enhanced relaxation procedure, using psychological principles to provide what can perhaps be described as a 'supercharged' technique due to its links with mental imagery techniques that will be discussed in Chapter 11.

Progressive muscle relaxation

Progressive muscle relaxation, or PMR, is a muscle-to-mind technique developed by Edmund Jacobson in 1938. Essentially, this technique involves tensing and then relaxing different muscle groups. If all of the muscle groups are relaxed, then there can be no tension in the body. As a consequence any tension in the mind should disappear. It is important that the performer knows the difference between these two opposing states. Awareness of muscular tension will act as the trigger for the performer to begin the relaxation technique. The table opposite provides practical instructions for PMR, but it may help to transfer the instructions into

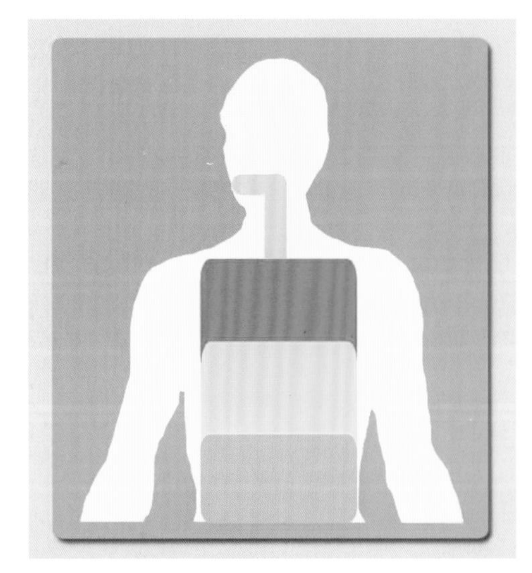

Illustration showing the hypothetical compartments of the lungs. (Boot-Handford/Author)

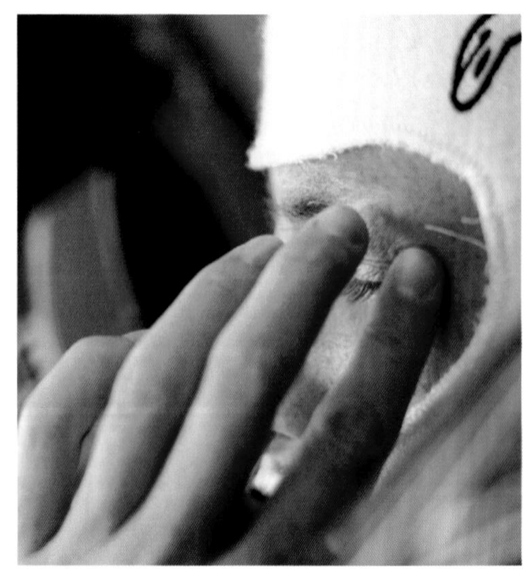

Directing attention to breathing patterns and mental images may increase relaxation. (LAT)

audio format so that you can play them back as you go through the exercise. Follow each step by tensing and relaxing each muscle group in turn. You should pay attention to the difference between tense and relaxed muscles. Each step should take approximately ten seconds.

Step	Instruction
1	Make yourself comfortable in a quiet environment. Remove or loosen any restrictive clothing. Breathe in deeply, hold and exhale. Do this two more times. You should begin to feel more relaxed.
2	If you hear any noises do not ignore them, but focus on inhaling and exhaling slowly.
3	Begin by tensing the muscles of your lower left leg and foot by pointing your toes. Hold this tension for five seconds and then relax. You can feel the difference between tension and relaxation in your calf and foot. Repeat this procedure once more. Do this for the left leg and then twice for the right leg and foot.
4	Move on to tensing the left thigh and buttocks. Tense the left thigh muscle and buttocks by pushing down into the floor. Hold this tension for five seconds and then relax. You can feel the difference between tension and relaxation in your left thigh and buttocks. Repeat this procedure once more. Do this for the left leg and then twice for the right thigh and buttocks.
5	Next, tense and relax the left bicep. Do this by bending at the elbow. Hold this tension for five seconds and then relax. You can feel the difference between tension and relaxation in your left bicep. Repeat this procedure once more. Do this for the left bicep and then twice for the right bicep.
6	Next, tense and relax the left forearm. Do this by making a fist. Hold this tension for five seconds and then relax. You can feel the difference between tension and relaxation in your left forearm. Repeat this procedure once more. Do this for the left forearm and then twice for the right forearm.
7	Move on to tensing and relaxing the muscles in your back. Do this by arching your back. Hold this tension for five seconds and then relax. You can feel the difference between tension and relaxation in your back muscles. Repeat this procedure once more. Next, tense and relax the muscles in your stomach and chest. Do this by inhaling, holding and releasing. Hold this tension for five seconds and then relax. You can feel the difference between tension and relaxation in your stomach and chest. Repeat this procedure once more.
8	Next, tense and relax the muscles in your neck and shoulders. Do this by shrugging your shoulders. Hold this tension for five seconds and then

relax. You can feel the difference between tension and relaxation in your neck and shoulder muscles. Repeat this procedure once more.

9 Move on to tensing and relaxing the muscles in your face and forehead. Do this by clenching your jaw and frowning. Hold this tension for five seconds and then relax. You can feel the difference between tension and relaxation in your facial muscles. Repeat this procedure once more.

10 Mentally scan your whole body for any tension. If there is any, release it by tension and relaxation.

11 Finally, focus on the relaxed feelings your muscles are now giving you. You are calm and relaxed.

12 Before getting up, it is important to return to a greater degree of conscious awareness. Count slowly, from 1–7, exhaling on every count. As you get closer to 7, you will feel more and more alert.

13 You should now feel completely relaxed and rejuvenated.

Adapted from Hodge (1994)

When you have mastered PMR you can dispense with the tension part of the technique. By this I mean that you can go straight to the relaxation steps, because you have already identified tension. This is where the benefits occur. If you are on the starting grid, with tense shoulders and one minute to go, there will not be enough time to run through the whole technique. Instead, you should simply feel the tension in your shoulders and run through the relaxation step for these muscles. Within a matter of seconds you should find that the tension dissipates and is replaced with relaxed shoulder and neck muscles. That done, it is time to regain focus, hone in to the first corner and wait for the lights to change.

Some competitors like to incorporate a key word, 'relax', into the technique at each stage, so you can modify the procedure to suit yourself. I shall discuss self-talk in Chapter 10, but the use of key words does suggest that links can be made between many psychological skills techniques in order to provide competitors with an effective – indeed, tailored – adaptation to suit their own specific requirements.

Autogenic training

Autogenic training is a mind-to-muscle technique developed in the 1930s by Johannes Schultz. The underlying concepts of autogenic training are the physical sensations of 'heaviness' and 'warmth'. Mental effort is directed towards a particular body part, in which a sensation of heaviness is induced. For example, I might instruct you to imagine your right calf becoming extremely heavy. I would then ask you to imagine the right calf losing its heaviness and becoming warm and sun-kissed. After successful practice I would progress by directing your attention toward 'coolness' in your forehead. The remaining element of this technique is to direct attention toward having a rhythmic breathing pattern and strong, stable heart rate. This technique is akin to self-hypnosis and rests on verbal instruction or internal thought processes. For example, 'My right calf is heavy; my right calf is relaxed and warm; my heart rate is slow and calm; my breathing is strong and rhythmic; and, my forehead is cool.' This technique takes a long time to develop to a high standard and, given that racers' schedules are usually rather hectic, is not ideal. However, it is available and may prove useful, so the message is to give it a try.

Meditation

Meditation is a centuries-old technique, aimed at eliciting relaxation. It has perhaps gained a certain stigma in modern society, due to its association with religious experiences or cults. To label it in this way would be unfair and one should remember that if it enhances performance there should be little concern about how it is used elsewhere in society.

The key to meditation is to adopt a passive approach. This means that rather than having an active mind, you should practise redirecting your attention towards a cue word. By focusing on a key word such as 'calm' or 'relaxed', you are able to let the active thoughts wash over you. This is similar to situations where everyone around you has been experiencing stress and you simply rise above the stress, coming out seemingly unscathed. The cue word enables you to do the same in meditation.

The table below provides basic instruction in achieving a meditative state:

Step	Instruction
1	Find a quiet environment and sit comfortably.
2	Shut your eyes.
3	Relax the muscles in your feet and move up through all muscle groups in the body, finishing at your facial muscles. Remain relaxed.
4	Focus on rhythmic breathing through your nose. Say the word 'calm' or 'relaxed' as you exhale. Be natural with your breathing cycle.
5	Continue doing this for up to 20 minutes.
6	When you are ready to finish, keep your eyes closed, sit quietly and let 'active' thoughts return to conscious awareness.
7	Open your eyes and remain seated for a few moments.

Adapted from Williams & Harris (2006)

Achieving a successful meditative state will take time and effort and should be practised regularly. It is important that you avoid practising shortly after a meal since the activity of your digestive system will interfere with achieving the relaxation response.

Meditation is an age-old Eastern technique. (Buckler/Author)

In practical terms meditation enables competitors to focus or switch attention selectively when required. It allows for the screening out of unwanted or undesirable information at appropriate moments. For example, consider the situation where you have come into the pits with a tyre problem. While you are waiting to go back onto the circuit for the final four minutes of qualifying, the mechanics are under pressure to deal with this problem urgently. At this point the last thing you should do is focus attention on the problem, or on the time left to overcome it. Rather, your focus should be elsewhere. By selectively attending to your key word of 'calm' or 'relaxed' you are freeing up your mind. You can be aware of, but unaffected by, the mechanics' progress. As they reach completion of the task you switch back to conscious reality, focus on the out-lap, and return to racing.

Sport psychologists continue to debate exactly how meditation exerts its effects and whether meditation affects performance directly or indirectly. I would tend to think that the effects are more likely to be indirect: meditation has an effect on reducing tension, stress and anxiety and these in turn appear to improve performance. However, this discussion is of little practical benefit on track. Put simply, if it works for you, use it. If it doesn't, then don't.

Biofeedback

Biofeedback has been considered to be a relaxation technique, but I also like to think of it as a way of using signs and signals from your body to check whether your strategies are working in your favour or against you. Although I discussed the fact that the autonomic nervous system is under involuntary control when I used the example of not having consciously to think about breathing, biofeedback works on the principle that we can exercise a certain element of control over the respiratory system. In order to do this, you need to be made aware of what to look for and recognise the correct signs. In a laboratory setting this would be achieved, for example, by recording the electromyogram (EMG), skin conductance response (SCR) and heart rate (HR), but such measurement techniques are largely

Heart rate monitors are inexpensive and effective tools for use in biofeedback training. (Author)

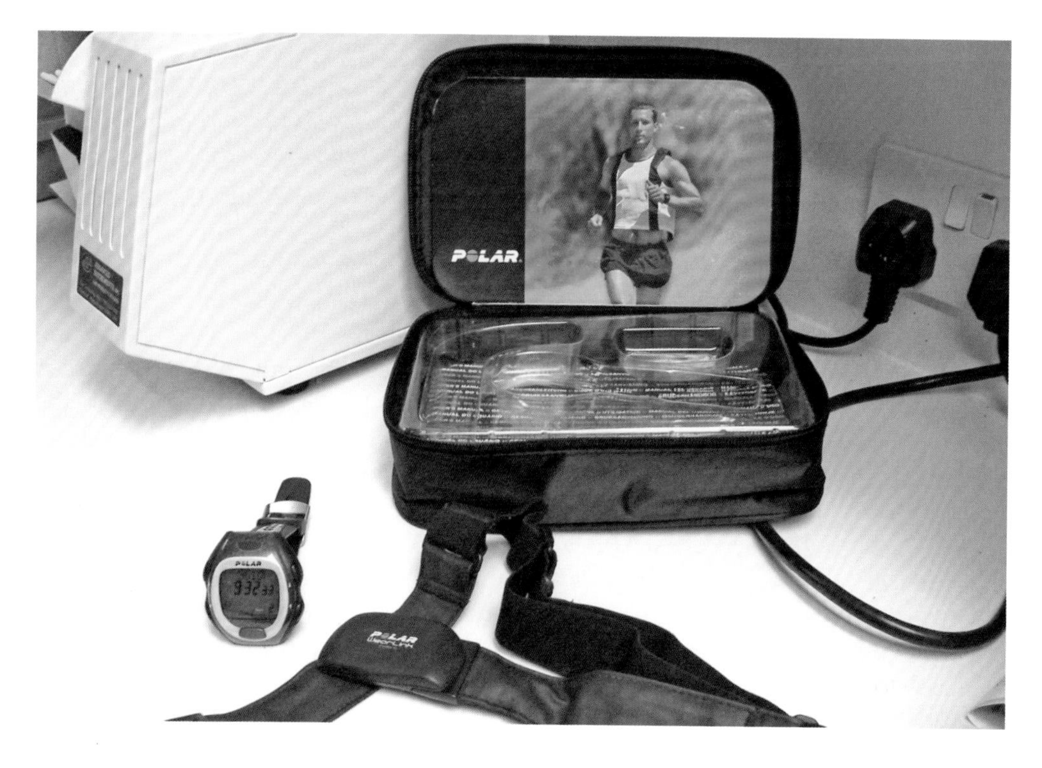

inaccessible to racers. However, biofeedback devices are readily accessible to us all following the advent of heart rate monitors, which can be purchased in most sport shops for no more than a few pounds. I would, however, recommend that if you are able to purchase a monitor with an infrared link to a computer the data can then be viewed and evaluated on screen at your leisure.

Essentially these monitors work through the use of a transceiver. Rather than using cumbersome and uncomfortable electrodes, the monitor is worn around the chest and picks up electrical signals from the heart. These signals are transmitted to a monitor worn on the wrist. Downloading to computer takes place in a similar way to the downloading of jpeg images from a digital camera. A software program usually produces a graphical representation of your heart rate data, which, with practice, can be easily interpreted. For those practitioners wishing to investigate this topic in greater detail I would recommend reading *Biofeedback Applications in Performance Enhancement* by Blumenstein, Bar-Eli and Tenenbaum (see Bibliography). The present chapter seeks only to synthesise and condense the information into manageable, practical segments.

When should relaxation techniques be used?

As I pointed out earlier, relaxation techniques should be used to combat somatic or cognitive anxiety. It is vital that you explore your optimal levels of arousal for peak performance. Imagine sitting in the pit garage before a championship-deciding race. You are running through a deep relaxation exercise and are now in such a state of relaxation that you are no longer ready to carry out the task in hand. In discussing relaxation with you, I might suggest finding out what level of arousal you need to perform successfully. This can be explored through discussion and examining performance during testing sessions or free practice. If you return saying that you were unable to retain focus or were 'having an off day', I might infer that the relaxation technique was employed at an inappropriate time before you went onto the circuit. We would have to adopt a calculated, although somewhat trial-and-error, method of finding the most opportune time to employ the technique. For this very reason, you should be practised in using relaxation techniques before you need to use them during important, competitive events.

It is, however, possible to keep an eye on proceedings during competition in order to identify when problems begin to emerge. Sport psychologists are usually experts in using observational techniques, which will enable them to pinpoint various occasions where tension and anxiety manifest themselves through a competitor's behaviour. I watched a competitor gently hitting the back of his machine because the mechanics were running behind schedule, which was making him late out of the pit garage. If there had been a jerrycan in the vicinity I feel certain that it would have received a frustrated kick! If this performer had been successfully practised in relaxation techniques at this point in his career, he would have refocused, reduced any tension and got on with his mental preparation.

During the 2002 World Superbike Season, Colin Edwards had just secured poll position in qualifying with four minutes left. Troy Bayliss was in his own pit garage watching the times. His crew told him that he had four minutes to take poll back. With that, he put on his helmet and gloves, jumped on his bike, rode the out-lap and then put in a flying lap to take poll with seconds to spare. This is the essence of relaxation techniques. If you only have a matter of seconds to prepare, then you need to be able to use a technique that can be adapted to suit the situation. Troy Bayliss's qualifying response exemplifies this idea.

It is common, amongst competitors I have worked with, for them to practise relaxation techniques during the days leading up to a race, before and after free practice, during qualifying and on race day itself. The message is quite simple: identify when it is necessary to relax and find the time and place to apply your relaxation technique. Relaxation is an important part of a competitor's preparation. If it is left out, or a half-hearted attempt is made, there can be no guarantees that performance will be successful. If, however, time and effort are allocated the possibilities are limited only by the competitor's confidence and racing ability.

If tension mounts while you are on the grid, you should feel the tension in your arms as you hold the wheel or grip the handlebars. Next, I would expect you to 'feel' the change to relaxation as you run through the PMR or autogenic technique. I would expect your heart rate to be reduced through your awareness of biofeedback. I certainly would *not* expect you to enter a 20-minute meditative state just before the lights go out for the start of the race.

Enhanced relaxation training

This section acts as a link between relaxation and mental imagery techniques (outlined in Chapter 11). John King, a psychiatrist from Worcestershire, developed a technique for use with patients who were referred to him suffering from depression. The technique, which he called 'enhanced relaxation training' (ERT), aimed to reduce or 'improve' the symptoms of depression by providing patients with a mental simulation of a seaside environment. Essentially, this clever technique involved sounds and smells of the coast, combined with the feel of sunshine (provided by heat lamps). King used mental imagery to underpin these stimuli, by talking his patients through a mental sequence of visual events at the seaside. The result was a mental imagery sequence that was lifelike for his patients. The technique rested on simple yet effective theory. In the main, people go on holiday to relax, unwind, recover from the stresses of daily life and return feeling refreshed. Nowadays, many racers live this kind of lifestyle outside of racing.

King assembled all of the relevant props to provide the context for a holiday in the privacy and safety of his consulting room and was able to manipulate the environment such that he could introduce feelings of calmness and relaxation in

Visual imagery containing relaxing destinations is useful in training your mind and body to unwind. (sutton-images.com)

his patients. He was then able to make suggestions about how the seaside seemed to be improving their mood and emotional feelings, thus providing these patients with a dilemma: if my mood has improved, how can I be depressed? You will recall a similar argument earlier in the chapter regarding anxiety and relaxation. Of course, I have simplified the situation considerably. However, it is only necessary to highlight the concept of what King was attempting to do. The message is simply that if you wish to get into a relaxation mindset, you should put as many 'props' in place as possible. Of course, I do not want you to think that combining mental imagery and relaxation training is only useful for combating depression. Rather, the use of mental imagery may be used to induce relaxation quickly and easily, with the power of verbal persuasion.

Having read this chapter you will begin to realise the significance of anxiety, stress, attention and concentration. Somatic and cognitive anxiety was discussed more fully in Chapter 5 in relation to stress, and in Chapter 2 in relation to attention and concentration. I would suggest that you read each of these chapters again and then return to this chapter to cement your understanding of how relaxation is intimately interlinked to these issues.

Chapter 10

Self-talk and cognitive restructuring

IN THE CHAPTER on relaxation I discussed muscle-to-mind and mind-to-muscle techniques. The present chapter stays with the concept of mind-to-muscle but discusses a cognitive technique that will help you to perceive your state of arousal in a positive, productive manner. You can use two techniques in order to do this: self-talk, your internal 'voice'; and cognitive restructuring, changing your thought patterns. Self-talk and cognitive restructuring can be thought of as two sides to the same coin: self-talk can only be successful if the thoughts in a competitor's head are positive. If those thoughts are negative, they can be changed or restructured to become positive. This, in essence, is what cognitive restructuring aims to do. The following examples will highlight my point.

The next time you are driving or riding on a clear road, with catseyes, a nice sweeping set of S-bends and good visibility, choose a line through them. Every time you cross the central line to position on the other side of the road, say to yourself, 'I must miss the catseyes, I must miss the catseyes,' as you return to your side of the road. There is a high probability that you will hit one of them. Now try the same manoeuvre, but this time, say, 'I must aim for the gap, I must aim for the gap'. You will more than likely miss the catseyes because you have 'told' your brain that the only thing that is important visually here, is the gap between the catseyes and not the catseyes themselves. Now we can apply the idea to the racetrack. If the way you perceive two competitors in front of you will have an effect on the outcome, then do not perceive their cars or bikes, but rather, where you want to be; the gap between them. If you aim for the space it will open up in your mind.

Let us now consider a specific racing example. Imagine that you are approaching the Coppice turn at Silverstone too quickly. If your mind is telling you that you will lose the back wheel slide that you are in, then you *will* lose it. If, on the other hand, your mind is telling you that you will regain full control, back your car or bike in and power through the corner, then the likelihood is that

Using positive self-talk is a good way of retaining focus and overcoming challenges. (David.WillowPhotography.co.uk)

you won't lose it. The self-talk taking place in your head to negotiate the slide and accelerate out of the corner may be something like, 'Balance ... balance ... balance ... bal ... lance ... power ... power ... *power*.' Indeed, my experience suggests that racers use self-talk a lot during motorsport and this is a good sign, because it is possible to build on their existing techniques.

However, self-talk can be, and usually is, also negative. To use the example above, it would not be uncommon to get into the back wheel slide and hear the self-talk voice saying 'Too fast ... too fast ... too fast.' On its own, this is no bad thing. The competitor's perception of the implications is the important element. The logical next step to 'Too fast' is to exit the track shortly afterwards.

What is self-talk?

Self-talk is the mental activity that occurs whenever an individual thinks and makes perceptions and beliefs conscious. It is talking in the mind rather than aloud. Self-talk helps you to stay focused on strategic elements of your competition. In practice you might use the word 'Now' to signify the exact moment in a race for you to make your overtaking move on a competitor who has been slowing you down for the last three laps. It is the equivalent of hitting the 'faster' switch, narrowing your focus, providing a shot of energy and leading to a successful racing manoeuvre.

When should self-talk be used?

Different types of self-talk exist, for different situations: correcting bad habits; refocusing; building self-confidence; controlling effort; and modifying arousal levels. You need to be aware of each of these to help you understand how the technique will be of use to you.

Correcting bad habits

This is rather like self-coaching or self-instruction. Here, self-talk is used to question how you are sitting, what your balance is like, whether you are maintaining control of your car or bike without tension creeping in and you becoming too brutal. Self-talk may be used to make corrections when you are learning a new skill and need to develop and refine it, such as backing into a corner, or feathering the throttle during a power-slide.

Refocusing

Cue words and statements such as 'be here', 'here and now' and any others you feel comfortable with are useful for bringing you back to the reality of now. Lyrics from favourite songs may help you here; for example, a line from Eminem

Positive self-talk helps in the decision-making process. (Ross Curnow/Stuart Patterson)

Positive self-talk helps you refocus after a racing incident. (David.WillowPhotography.co.uk)

encapsulates this nicely – 'Lose yourself in the moment ... you own it ... once in a lifetime ... never let go'. From this, I would select the 'you own it' piece to mean 'I own the track in front of me'. Be careful in your selection: for instance, 'Help' by the Beatles is not recommended!

Building self-confidence

Self-confidence is a vital element of successful performance. Competitors who lack it are immediately disadvantaged and face an uphill battle. If you are lacking in self-confidence you may enhance it, indirectly, through self-talk. Self-confidence was discussed in greater depth in Chapter 4.

Controlling effort

Having focused on the task in hand, it is important that racers stay tuned. Self-talk can be used to keep the level of effort high, avoiding any lapses in performance. Indeed, the phrases 'stay in tune' and 'stay on the pace' are good examples that help to control effort levels. As a safety net, refocusing should be used if effort does falter too much. When the call comes through on the radio to push harder, a driver might be forgiven for getting rather frustrated. Indeed, Jenson Button made the point during an informal interview, with his response: 'What do you *think* I'm doing?' If you are content that you are controlling your effort, then such a 'request' from the pits will not irritate you. A good self-talk response to 'Push harder' would be something like, 'I will push more and more so long as it feels right for me to do so.'

Modifying arousal levels

Self-talk can be used to psyche yourself up or calm yourself down. Essentially it is used to control your arousal level depending on how nervous you are and whether the level of arousal is facilitative or debilitative. This also depends on how you perceive the excitement or arousal and how it is linked to your changes in mood. If you do not feel in the right frame of mind to race, you can use self-talk to alter your present mood-state. Find out what the problem is, seek the solution, and then use self-talk to confirm that you are moving towards that solution.

Every action begins with a thought. Consequently, if you think positively then you will get used to acting positively. You might start by telling yourself that you believe you can do it and that you have been practising it with some success in training. Then you can continue with you know you can do it, backed up with the knowledge of the training preparation.

Eventually your confidence will increase as well. Sometimes others may mistake this confidence for arrogance, but this could merely be extreme confidence overflowing into speech. In the sports world, competitors who use positive self-talk persist in their exercise regimes. Consequently self-talk has the additional bonus of helping to retain or increase motivation when the going gets tougher than normal.

How should self-talk be used?

By its very nature of being an internal voice, self-talk cannot be measured directly. Nevertheless, this is not a problem for sport psychologists. We must ensure however, that you understand how to use self-talk and how to measure progress if it is used. It is also important to explain that negative thoughts may lead to your experiencing a mental block, which could have a detrimental effect on performance.

Although the methods outlined below are subjective, a check can be made at opportune moments to establish whether or not it is working adequately. I will outline three methods for using self-talk in training for competition. You should decide which one works best for you, or whether a combination of methods provides a useful variation on the theme.

Looking back at previous races helps remind you of your thoughts and self-talk at the time. (Rimstock plc)

Retrospection

Think back to very good and not so good performances. Try to recall your pre- and post-performance thoughts and feelings – you can use videotapes of the performance to help prompt these. It is important to remember, however, that using recall methods can lead to distorted and inaccurate incidents. Psychologists know from research that our memory is not always as accurate as we think it is. If you start to keep a racing log or journal you can use this information in the future when you need to look back. If I ask you to recall events from a particular race three years ago, you may struggle; but if you kept records you could give me all the information I need, even down to the weather conditions and track temperature at the time. That particular race might be the key to overcoming existing difficulties this season.

Imagery

Recreate performances or sequences mentally, as will be discussed in Chapter 11. Once again, it is necessary, therefore, to recall and record thoughts and feelings associated with the competition, using it to remember the positive self-talk before and after the event.

Self-talk logs

Keep daily records of any self-talk that you have carried out during competitions and make a note of what the situation was when you carried out that self-talk. This also helps you to assess whether you are predominantly positive or negative in your self-talk. I carefully log all details of my training rides when cycling so that I can assess why certain rides were not as fast, or why average speeds may have been higher or lower than usual. I even keep a record of wind direction and which type of fluid I used on the ride. These logs help me to 'push harder' but also give me explanations if my performance dips.

Patterns of self-talk

It is essential that you identify patterns of self-talk before you can develop a technique for personal use. Several methods exist, including: thought stopping; visual cues; and physical signals.

Thought stopping

It is possible to use a thought or cue to interrupt unwanted thoughts as they occur. You can quickly say out loud 'Stop!' as soon as you know you are saying or thinking an undesirable thought. It is important that you consider the thought, if there is time, and evaluate and reflect on it, but then you need to insert another, more positive thought in its place.

An image of a red traffic light instructs you to stop a negative thought. (sutton-images.com)

Visual cues

You can use a visual cue, such as a mental picture of a red traffic light, representing 'stop'. Again, you will need quickly to insert another, more positive thought in place of the negative one and then change the red traffic light to green.

Physical signals

You can use a physical movement such as snapping your fingers to represent 'Stop'. Yet again, you need quickly to insert another more positive thought. Of course, this is not as easy to do on a motorcycle, but you might nudge your boot on the foot peg instead.

Practical Task

The task below will help you to identify where self-talk may help you. Follow the instructions, decide how many of them are in your control, and work on putting positive self-talk statements in place to overcome any challenges you have identified.

Instruction

1. Recall a qualifying session or race in which you felt you could have produced a more successful performance.
2. Write down what you did, what you felt, and what you said. Look critically at your narrative for negative thoughts. How could you change some of the negative thoughts? Are there some areas where you are thinking positively? Try not to punish yourself for these; give yourself some credit!
3. List ten of your most common thoughts when you are competing and performing.
4. Look at the list you have produced. Have you focused on issues outside of your control? Have you been unduly negative?
5. For every thought, write a positive statement or a self-focused alternative.
6. All you need to do now is to recognise when negative thinking occurs and insert the new positive thought in its place!

Self-talk should become automatic or second nature

As I pointed out in Chapter 2, if a competitor thinks too much about what they are doing, these very thought processes might distract them from the task by disrupting the automatic performance of a skill. I wholeheartedly agree with this. However, self-talk is about key words or phrases. It is mentally economical and it feeds into your race strategy. As soon as you begin to focus too much on exactly how it feels to feather the throttle through turn 3 your attention will be diverted and you will begin to make mistakes. You should be aiming to be able to use self-talk automatically rather than having to think too much about it. In order to do this you have to go through the process of thinking too much about it. I recall being mid-bend recently, going too fast and being on the limit. Automatically, a bellowing voice came from inside me, 'Don't!' In a single word, I had given myself guidance on not lifting the throttle, not braking, not panicking, not being distracted, but instead on focusing purely on exiting the turn on the tarmac and not eating hedgerow! If this automatic, internal response had not happened, I would have crashed. This takes practice. Take the challenge.

Cognitive restructuring: how to get the most from your inner voice

Arguably, none of us see the world as it really is. Instead, we *perceive* the world – we see it as we think it exists for us. These mental images of the same piece of track show how two racers might perceive the situation differently. This is based on the way we think, our attitudes, beliefs, superstitions and stereotypes, etc.

Cognitive restructuring is derived from a psychotherapy technique developed back in the 1960s by Albert Ellis. Basically, it aims to direct us towards modifying self-defeating, irrational and anxiety-provoking cognitions or thoughts. It can be used to restructure these thoughts and to alter irrational or 'bad' thoughts. It is relatively easy to spot negative thoughts and substitute them with positive thoughts before they get too serious. With practice you will stop negative thoughts before they emerge. There should be nothing negative in your head when you are racing, regardless of what is happening. Instead, you will have plenty of things to keep your focus. A combination of cognitive restructuring with self-talk can be used to provide self-reward and to increase your effort.

When should you use cognitive restructuring?

Cognitive restructuring can be used in various situations. For example, it is effective in reducing anxiety and increasing levels of coping under adverse conditions. It is also useful in increasing self-confidence, as well as the motivation to train or perform. If you have trouble with your winter running schedule, for instance, then perhaps cognitive restructuring can help you to think differently about your fitness programme.

Stages in developing cognitive restructuring

Cognitive restructuring is not as difficult as it may initially appear. It typically comprises four stages. You need to be aware that your beliefs, perceptions and assumptions influence emotional arousal. Consider the perceptions of a racing incident, from the point of view of two competitors who have just taken each other out on the track. If either competitor feels anger, this results from his or her perception of what has just happened. You should identify underlying ideas in your racing in order to recognise any potential irrational, self-defeating foundations you may have, such as 'I will never be able to make a successful block-pass at the esses,' or 'He always does better than I do at this circuit.' Once you have identified these irrational thoughts, you need actively to criticise them, replacing them with thoughts that prevent or reduce maladaptive anxiety. Finally, you should practise and rehearse new thoughts, applying them to relevant racing situations.

You might like to use the following four questions to guide you in deciding whether the thoughts are irrational or distorted. I use these questions, based on sport psychology literature, because they are practical and elicit almost immediate responses from competitors.

Are the beliefs based on objective reality?
Do the thoughts help you reach your short- and long-term goals?
Are the thoughts helpful or self-destructive?
Do the thoughts reduce emotional conflict with yourself or others?

Having established that some thoughts may be irrational or distorted, you should list them on a sheet of paper, in no specific order. The table below provides some examples of irrational thoughts. I have headed the left-hand column 'self-defeating thought' in order to use the phrase 'self-enhancing thought' for the cognitively restructured thought. You may identify with these, or you may be able to list your own examples.

Self-defeating thought	**Self-enhancing thought**
I can't believe it is raining. I have to ride in the rain.	No one likes the rain but I can ride as well in it as anyone else.
You idiot.	Ease off. Everyone makes mistakes. Shrug it off and turn your mind to what you want to do.
I have no natural talent.	I've seen riders and drivers who had to work hard to be successful. I can improve if I practise correctly.
We'll win the race only if I keep up fast lap times.	Stop worrying about the times; just concentrate on how you're going to execute the lap.
I don't want to fail.	Nothing was ever gained by being afraid to take risks. As long as I give my best I'll never be a failure.
I got that corner completely wrong.	I will try a different line next lap.
I don't want to crash.	I have many things to focus on to ride successfully. I don't have room to think about crashes.

With practice you will be able to free your mind of unwanted thoughts. (Kevin F York Motorsport)

Once you have listed any negative thoughts that you may have before, during or after a session in the car or on the bike, it then becomes relatively straightforward to use the examples of self-enhancing thoughts listed above to restructure any negative thoughts that you have identified.

It is imperative that you believe these new thoughts. Anything less than total belief will be met with failure. I would also ask you to identify key words or phrases that will help you to keep focused and motivated during free practice, qualifying and race sessions. These might include: 'Come on!'; 'Yes!'; 'That felt good'; 'I have this/I can do it/I'm on it'; 'Smooth!'; 'Calm'; and 'Breathe' or 'Slow heart rate'.

This section has provided examples of self-enhancing thoughts that you might use to fend off self-defeating thoughts before they happen. If any creep in, you must address them rationally in relation to other things that are working positively. Your anxiety levels should remain comfortable.

Chapter 11

Mental imagery and visualisation

VISUALISATION IS SEEING A PICTURE of an event or sporting task in your mind. Mental imagery takes this picture and converts it into a sequence in your mind, much like playing a DVD inside your head. At a simple level visualisation may simply involve the storage of a single picture or basic moving image, *eg* of a circuit or a stadium. In contrast, mental imagery is an active, dynamic process, in which the image is continuously modified as if it were an enhanced video recording. You may already use this technique. Many racers believe that they know a circuit in their minds. The question you should ask yourself is, are you able to 'see' a picture (visualisation), or a video (mental imagery)? You may have a visual image of the circuit, but there is so much more that you could include to make it real.

As I showed with imagery-related relaxation in Chapter 9, other senses may be utilised to enhance the quality of the internal experience.

You may adopt one of two perspectives: internal or external. It is important to discover whether you adopt a perspective where you experience imagery from the point of view of being yourself seen within the image, or whether you experience it from within, looking outwards as it were.

In practical terms, common consensus in the literature is that competitors may benefit from employing imagery techniques. Although the exact mechanism remains speculative, the mere perception in your head of 'having been there before' seems to pay dividends when you attend an event in physical reality.

What is visualisation?

The clue to answering this question is evident in the root of the word: visual. Visualisation involves a picture being stored in the mind – *eg* the Craner Curves at Donington Park or the Bus Stop chicane at Spa – this 'picture' being the internal equivalent of a photograph or jpeg image on a computer screen. While it may be useful in evoking memories that accompany the image, it is far from the real deal.

Can you see every inch of the circuit in your mind? (Author)

A more complex version of visualisation may be of the same location played as a video, again only using the visual sense. Although this is arguably closer to reality than the photograph-based equivalent, it still lacks the complexity necessary for a lifelike representation of it to be stored in the human brain.

As I have said elsewhere, humans are visually dominant. If you take the time to reflect on how important sight is to your own daily life and, indeed, your passion for motorsport, you can understand why there is such a heavy reliance on the visual sense. Nevertheless, this leaves a wealth of untapped information provided by other sensory systems that can be incorporated into visualisation to provide a higher quality experience. This is where mental imagery goes a step further.

What is mental imagery?

Robert Weinberg and Daniel Gould suggest that 'imagery is actually a form of simulation ... similar to a real sensory experience (*eg* seeing, feeling or hearing), but the entire experience occurs in the mind' (Weinberg and Gould, 1999, p.266). You may not realise, but you may readily identify with this. Consider the occasions when you have been slower through a corner in free practice than an opponent, only to think, 'If I watch and take the opponent's line I should also go through the corner as quickly.' At the end of the session, having obtained the information, you might retire to your motorhome or pit garage and practise taking the desired line through the corner in your mind, over and over again until it becomes second nature. Of course, if you are able to do this for all sections of the track where you are not content with your line, then you may, for example, end the next day's qualifying session 0.9 of a second quicker than your free practice time. This may in actuality put you six places higher on the starting grid, such is the potential for the effective use of mental imagery.

The idea that other senses can be incorporated into mental imagery is not surprising. The human brain comprises many systems and sub-systems, all of which communicate in some way with each other, whether this is directly or indirectly. Indeed, if you look out of the window at this very moment and see a vehicle go past you will more than likely also hear that vehicle. The brain does not store these pieces of information as two separate perceptions. Rather, they are combined. Why not, therefore, use the senses to your advantage when creating a mental image? The more detail you can add, the more realistic the experience will become.

When we talk of mental imagery, we are therefore concerned with so much more than just the visual system. In order to avoid any misleading or confusing subtleties in terminology, I would favour the term 'mental rehearsal' to encompass all aspects of acquiring, developing and refining a mental representation of a forthcoming task or competition.

How does imagery work?

The exact mechanism behind imagery remains elusive. Nevertheless, imagery seems to convince your brain that imagining a situation is synonymous with reality. This is conveniently illustrated through dreaming. For example, you may have had the fairly common 'I'm late' dream. You have an important appointment or competition tomorrow and you suddenly wake up in a cold sweat during the

Pay attention to fine detail and include this in your mental imagery. (Author)

night, because you have been dreaming about missing the alarm clock, getting up late, finding your vehicle won't start, getting stuck in traffic and not reaching the event on time. This, of course, is all taking place in your subconscious mind. Nevertheless, it is sufficiently 'real' to elicit physiological changes in your autonomic nervous system, such that you wake in a panic. Essentially, therefore, the events in your mind are 'real' until your conscious mind wakes and evaluates the reality of the situation, *ie* it is in fact 2:00am and you have plenty of time.

Sport psychologists are not entirely certain how imagery works and many theories exist. However, for our purposes we can take selected elements of each theory and apply it to motorsport for practical purposes:

- ***Psycho-neuro-muscular patterns*** – Stored psycho-neuro-muscular patterns are thought to be identical to those patterns that exist in response to actual events. This means that the way in which you think helps your brain to access the correct muscular pattern that is needed. So, the more you practise the action mentally, the stronger the connection and the quicker you will access it when needed. Imagery can also lead to an increase in electrical activity in the muscles associated with the task. If I were to attach EMG electrodes to your arms or legs and ask you to run through gear-change sequences in your mind, we would be able to record some muscular activity in the relevant muscles (though they are not moving). Mental rehearsal of this kind is akin to using a route map to discover how to get to a destination and then to practise it mentally until it becomes second nature.
- ***Symbolic learning*** – It may be that thoughts/cognition rather than electrical activity in the muscles is responsible. A 'blueprint' is formed, highlighting all possible solutions to a response. You simply need to select the correct solution from the blueprint and execute that response. A cognitively-based task involving strategy, such as executing the correct route through a complex circuit, would be best suited to the symbolic learning theory.
- ***Bio-information*** – Bio-information is the storage of two types of information in the brain: stimulus characteristics and response characteristics. These resemble computer programmes that work on an 'if X happens, then do Y' principle. Response characteristics are said to describe how you respond to the stimuli in the given situation. Physiological responses are particularly important here. Bio-informational theory holds that you need to incorporate both types of characteristics into your imagery so that you can develop, amend and strengthen them.
- ***Attention-arousal setting*** – This refers to how imagery can be used to increase attention, improve concentration, heighten focus, and mentally prepare for battle. It is about accessing all available sensory information, combining it, and using it to focus your attention and arousal level on the job of racing.

By putting all these elements together, you might, for example, imagine your heart rate increasing as a race gets ever closer. You might 'feel' some tension in your arms as you climb on board the bike or get into your race car. You might 'feel' clammy hands before exiting the pit garage for the warm-up lap. You might incorporate the sounds of the crowd and how the noise makes you feel. Does it increase anxiety or does it provide confidence? Similarly, how do you feel about your elevated heart rate? Does it make you feel anxious and tense, or does it give you a feeling of supreme energy and power to do the job in hand? Psychologically speaking, if you incorporate positive elements into your imagery these will inspire confidence in your ability to succeed. In refining the imagery you should expect to 'lose' the tension and clamminess and adjust your elevated heart rate to an optimal level. In short, you are completely ready for racing. You are doing with your head what your mechanics are aiming to do with the bike or car: achieve the perfect set-up.

It is worth noting at this point that the vital element of bio-informational theory is that the imagery resulting from your development of stimulus and response characteristics is specific to you: it is a mental 'fingerprint', unique to you and based on the cognitive meaning you assign to the characteristics. Your 'fingerprint' might not work for your competitors because they may be thinking differently about the situation.

Again, we return to the importance of strategy. Mental imagery can help to formulate your strategy for a race. For example, the concentration and attentional

Your engineers are working on the ideal race set-up, just as you are working on the ideal psychological set-up. (Aston Martin Racing)

focus required to execute a successful hot lap in qualifying is arguably very different from that required to execute the same lap in a 60-lap race situation. Mental imagery should be different for and specific to each situation, and you need to be able to distinguish the differences between them. This will enable you to develop a suitable imagery sequence for each one, which you will then be able to practise so that you can execute the appropriate reaction when you are racing. If this is a qualifying session, it goes without saying that the qualifying imagery information is required. I have spent time working on mental imagery with a rider in 600cc Supersport, in the British Superbike Championship. At a recent race meeting several members of the team came to me rather concerned that he had seemingly fallen asleep on his chair minutes before the race. Upon glancing over from a distance I could see that he was, in fact, riding the track in his mind, behaviour that looked to the untrained observer as if he was nodding off. He was using imagery to help focus his mind and concentrate on where he was riding, all before he got onto his race bike. This 'setting' of the mind would seem to be similar to flicking the 'I am ready' switch that puts you into optimal performance mode.

It seems, therefore, that there are several different pieces to the jigsaw, and you need to consider exactly how you might prepare for a successful performance. I shall discuss some of these jigsaw pieces as the chapter progresses.

Operationalising imagery

In practical terms, it is possible to use mental imagery in three different yet complementary ways:

- In learning and developing physical skills, such as the heel-and-toe technique in driving, or perhaps counter-steering in motorcycling. The physical elements of any sport can be rehearsed mentally if the necessary information is available.
- In developing psychological skills, such as reducing anxiety or psyching up. This ought to be useful in situations where a racer needs to deal with pressure.
- In developing and refining perceptual skills, such as taking the best line through a corner, or having to adapt that line because of an oil patch on the exit of the chicane.

Which perspective: internal or external imagery?

An internal perspective shows a view as if you are looking through a video camera's viewfinder. It is an eyeline perspective from behind the lens. The operator of the camera would never be 'in' the image because they are behind it. In contrast, an external perspective is such that the person holding the camera can be seen.

It is widely regarded that performers either create imagery in which they see themselves in a situation (an external perspective), or they see the situation as if it were from their own eyes (an internal perspective). A working example, using the pit garage theme, from earlier in this chapter, highlights these differences. If you adopt an external perspective, you might take your perspective from the pit wall, looking into the pit garage, where you see your bike or car, the mechanics and equipment. You see a chair, a helmet, some gloves and someone dressed in a race suit. You see the person pick up their helmet, place it on their head, fasten it and flip the visor, before picking up the gloves and putting them on. You see the person walk confidently towards the bike or car and get ready to exit the garage. Of course, the person you are looking at is yourself. Interestingly, research suggests that this perspective is more likely to be adopted by non-elite performers. Nevertheless, if you are lacking in confidence this perspective will do you no harm whatsoever.

If you adopt an internal perspective, it will be as if you are looking from behind your own eyes, looking out of and around the pit garage, where you see the bike or car, the mechanics and equipment. You see a chair, a helmet, and some gloves. You see your own hand pick up your helmet, and feel yourself place it on your head, fasten it and flip the visor, before seeing and feeling your hands picking up the gloves and putting them on. You see the distance to the bike or car getting shorter as you walk towards it and get ready to exit the garage. I could spend the next few pages enhancing this explanation, but I am sure that the message is now clear. Research suggests that this perspective is more likely to be held by elite performers and suggests that observing oneself is of lesser importance than executing the task successfully.

The decision regarding which perspective you should adopt would inevitably depend upon the underlying reasons for using imagery. For example, if you need to rehearse your routine mentally, in order to familiarise yourself with the competition, reduce potential stressors and suchlike, then it may be preferable to adopt an internal perspective. If, on the other hand, you need to boost self-confidence, then adopting an external perspective would enable you to 'see' yourself performing successfully in the situation. As a result this may do a lot to maintain, or indeed boost, self-confidence in advance of the actual competition.

If anything, external imagery is arguably more difficult to achieve successfully than internal imagery. While non-elite competitors may be more likely to use it, it does not automatically follow that the information is sufficiently refined to enhance performance. Consequently, it is vital that you practise each perspective. It is dangerous to assume that you already possess sufficient imagery skills, even if you believe that you use imagery. You should carry out an audit of your imagery. Do you use all senses? If not, why not? If you do, then are you including the level of detail covered in this chapter? You should then develop and refine these skills before practising using the correct tool for the job. For example, I would not advocate using external imagery if a racer's self-confidence is high as this may lead to psychological conflicts with motivational issues, which I discuss elsewhere in this book.

Using all of the senses to enhance imagery

As I mentioned above, humans are a visually dominant species. As a result one might argue that we have become rather complacent. If the information you receive from your visual system is sufficient for you to do the job, then why waste valuable time and energy in acquiring information from other senses? Of course, this is not strictly the case. The human brain constantly receives information from all sensory systems. However, it does not necessarily process all of it at the same level or in the same depth. Nevertheless, it is possible, with practice, to train the brain in processing information that is relevant to the task in hand. In short, the more usable information one has the easier, and indeed more appropriate, the decision becomes. The only time that this situation becomes detrimental is when the information is meaningless, and if this happens an inappropriate choice of decision is made. In real terms, this might mean the difference between staying on the racing line and exiting the track into the tyre wall.

So, what information might the other senses provide? The next time you go to the race circuit, start to become aware of what your senses are telling you. What can you see? You should be able to see information about the track and your competitors – how close an opponent is; the patch of oil on the racing line; the damp patch on the approach to turn 2; pit board information; marshals waving flags; and many other, contextually relevant pieces of information. What can you hear? You may be able to hear information about how close an opponent is; whether they have reached the rev-limiter; whether their car or bike (or, indeed, your own) is firing on all cylinders; tyre-squeal or whether the tyre is spinning up, and so on. What can you feel physically? You may feel the tyres spinning; adhesion levels diminishing; under-steer or over-steer; information from your arms about cornering forces etc. What can you smell? You may be able to smell smoke coming from your engine, which has just blown and is dumping oil on the track; excessively hot brakes; or simply something that was not there before and indicates some sort of problem for you. The gustatory, or taste, sense plays little if any role in providing information in a motorsport environment. However, some competitors might notice a 'dry mouth' sensation before the lights turn green. A dry mouth is quite natural under such circumstances and is part of the human body's 'fight-or-flight' mechanism.

You may identify with any, most or all of these examples. If they have happened in reality, then why not incorporate them into your mental imagery? In doing so you will be providing yourself with imagery as lifelike as the real thing, but in your head. You can rehearse this imagery until it becomes second nature and, if the underlying theory holds true, you will be strengthening the functionally

Life-like mental imagery is thought to strengthen connections in the brain. (LAT)

equivalent connections within your brain so that you can make the right choice at the right time and be completely familiar with it.

As this section highlights, if a competitor incorporates information provided by various senses into his or her mental imagery, the imagery should be vivid and of high quality. This is hardly surprising, given that although the human brain comprises many systems, it is also a part of a system. Consequently the brain processes information from a variety of interdependent sub-systems, such as the senses, the endocrine system (responsible for hormone release), the cardiovascular system (responsible for fluctuations in heart rate) and the autonomic nervous system (responsible for the stress response) to name but a few. This interdependence also operates for psychological skills techniques. For example, combining mental imagery with relaxation can be extremely powerful.

Effective use of mental imagery skills

At least three key issues emerge if mental imagery is to be used effectively in preparation for competition: belief; lucidity or vividness; and control.

Belief

At an early point in proceedings it is vital to recognise that mental imagery will only aid preparation for an event if you believe in it. Let's face it, if I ask you to do something that you don't have any faith in it is unlikely to work. If I can show you by helping you to obtain your own examples of it working, then you are more likely to accept the technique and benefit from its use.

Lucidity or vividness

I have already discussed the importance of acquiring information from many sources for incorporation into mental imagery. A lucid piece of mental imagery contains high-quality, detailed information of varying levels of significance. It is as close to the real thing as one can get but is in the mind.

Consider how successful computer games have become since technology has enabled programmers to re-create so-called reality within the game: you can get so involved in a game that your brain is deceived into believing that you are actually part of it. Mental imagery is the equivalent of the most realistic computer game, but can be made even better. Consider the many hours you may have spent playing a racing game in order to learn the circuit, only to find that when you exit Paddock Hill Bend at Brands Hatch the real track drops away from you and you have that 'That didn't happen in the game' sensation. I could quote numerous other examples here, but I am certain that you can identify with what I am saying. In the Paddock Hill Bend example, I would build how it feels to exit this corner into my mental imagery sequence. Of course, I can only include this kind of detail after I have completed some sighting laps. My advice, therefore, would be to use the computer game to provide an awareness of the direction the circuit takes, but then to ride or drive the track for real, picking up the pieces of information not contained in the game. Oh yes, and remember that the game may not be up to date in terms of new circuit modifications.

Control

Control is a vital yet sometimes overlooked aspect of mental imagery. If you have practised the circuit, and every time you went round turn 6 you ran wide, there is a danger that you may incorporate this error into your mental imagery. Consequently you *will* run wide every time you practise mentally and every time you practise for real. It is imperative that you are able to control the imagery to your advantage. It will help you to image the outcome that you want, rather than the events leading to a less satisfactory outcome. Sport psychologists generally agree that stressful situations are made worse when there is no element of control and this may lead to a phenomenon known as 'learned helplessness'. In short, if you always run wide in practice you simply accept that it will happen time and time again. But I would argue that it is possible, through controlling your mental imagery, to achieve the desired outcome. For example, you are more likely to get through a corner that if you have entered too hot if you imagine yourself getting round it than you imagine yourself exiting the track. Of course, the laws of physics will inevitably conspire against you in the most extreme situations, but belief may, just *may*, get you out of trouble. As a competitor, your desire to never give up is evident all the time. Do not lose sight of this when you are in the situation I describe above.

So if you are losing grip midway through a turn, how will it feel? How will you control your imagery so that you can rehearse getting out of the situation? In effect what you are doing is rehearsing worst-case scenarios, so that if they happen in real life you are practised in dealing with them.

Control of imagery is possibly the hardest thing to master and it takes practice. Do not be disheartened if you need to spend a little longer than expected on this aspect of the technique. It will pay dividends in the long run.

More examples of imagery in motorsport

Of course, it is very easy for me to sit here at my desk, on a peaceful summer's morning, providing advice on how to plan for a competition, or how to rehearse a race. In racing, nothing is ever as clear-cut as this. Nevertheless, it now becomes possible to develop a store of imagery appropriate to different 'what if?' situations. For instance, you might consider your closest rivals in the championship and reflect, objectively, on what they may do during the competition and develop a variety of possible scenarios thus: 'If he or she does X, I will do Y or Z. If he or she does A, I will do B or C.' In working terms, perhaps your opponent has decided to drive or ride a defensive line through the corner because they know they are slower than you, just as Lewis Hamilton did in blocking Kimi Räikkönen's Ferrari before turn 1 at the start of the British Grand Prix in 2007.

Your action might be to consider a passing manoeuvre on the outside, or to hang back and overtake them coming out of the turn. In terms of an imagery script, you might develop both scenarios and then pull out the appropriate one at the appropriate time. If your opponent does something different to your rehearsed scenarios, then it is easier to adapt to the reality of the situation by drawing upon the closest approximation in your mental armoury.

Having discussed the theory behind mental imagery, it is necessary at this point to move on to the practicalities of developing and practising mental imagery. The starting point for this is thinking about and writing an imagery script.

Writing an imagery script

Before beginning to help you to write an imagery script, it is important to establish how successfully you can create a mental image at the moment. The sample questions opposite are derived from the *Sport Imagery Questionnaire* (Hall, Mack, Paivio, and Hausenblas, 1998). You should answer the questions and then revisit them after you have developed your imagery technique. You will then be able to assess your progress.

Tick the box on the right if your answer to each question is 'yes'. The more boxes you are able to tick, the more successful you are at mental imagery. Remember to be honest!!

Can I 'see' the crowd celebrating my performance?
Can I 'see' other racers congratulating me on a good race?
Can I 'see' myself on the podium?
Can I 'feel' the 'atmosphere' of standing on the podium?
Can I 'see' myself being interviewed as a champion?
Can I 'feel' the atmosphere of winning a championship?
Can I 'feel' myself getting 'psyched up' for the race?
Can I 'feel' the excitement associated with the race?
Can I 'feel' the emotions I experience leading up to and during a race?
Can I adapt or change an image of a racing skill/technique?
Can I mentally make corrections to physical skills?
Can I consistently imagine performing racing techniques and skills successfully in my mind?
Before attempting a particular skill, can I imagine myself performing it perfectly?
Can I 'see' alternative strategies in case my race strategy fails?
Can I make up new race strategies in my head?
Can I 'see' each sector of a race?
Can I 'see' myself continuing with my race strategy even when 'under performing'?
Can I 'see' myself successfully following a race strategy?
Can I imagine myself being in control in difficult situations during a race?
Can I 'see' myself 'focusing in' during challenging situations?
Can I 'see' myself successfully overcoming challenging situations?
Can I 'see' myself giving 100% during a race?
Can I imagine myself appearing self-confident in front of other racers?

Use this chapter to help you develop your imagery for any boxes left unticked. You may also use the chapter to help in enhancing the vividness and clarity of your mental imagery. In doing so, you will be recreating and practising these situations in your mind, remaining calm, focused and in control of your thoughts/feelings.

Having established your existing level of imagery ability, this information can be used to help develop an imagery script. It would be unwise, however, to launch straight into writing the imagery script before I have given you an idea of what is and is not important in the environment. To do this I would like you to start by taking a mental journey around your living room.

Try to picture the shape of the room, the location of furniture, television, fireplace, tables etc. Then I would like you to picture the colour of the walls, and the location of mirrors, prints or photographs. Picture the location of any windows or doors and the view through these. A basic representation of your living room should now be emerging in your mind. When you are happy that you can picture the scene, it is necessary to add increasing levels of detail. Picture the colour of the carpet or floor covering. Has the sun faded it in patches? Are there any coffee or other stains on it and is it frayed anywhere? If you are unable to answer these questions, have a look the next time you are in the living room, check them and incorporate the new information into the image. You can also add the colour of the walls, damaged areas, the position of light switches and perhaps radiators. Next might be the visual texture of the walls and whether the prints or photographs are hanging straight or skewed. Your mental image is now beginning to build to a high degree of complexity. If you build the picture in this way, it becomes possible to take this to the finest level of detail. The point is to show you how powerful the technique can be as you pick up more and more information from the environment. I tend to concentrate only on the visual system for the living room example, and pay less attention to other senses.

Now that you are ready to move on to mental imagery for the racing circuit, we can include your other senses. An example might include asking you to feel how

Begin to practise by imagining walking around your own home. (Author)

comfortable the seat is under your buttocks or how well it supports the lumbar region of your back. If you are a rider, can you feel the tank between your thighs? If you are a driver, can you feel the seat belt around your shoulders?

Select a circuit about which you are already knowledgeable. Think of the different levels of complexity from the practice task above and start to build a mental imagery sequence of a lap around the selected circuit. The example below, provided by a motorcycle racer, highlights this:

> Accelerating from the apex of Goddard's, I line up with the outside kerb, parallel with the last quarter of the kerb on the right of the track.
> I pass under the bridge, heading for the left-hand side of the track, parallel with the pit lane as I approach Redgate.
> I use the end of the pit lane as my braking marker and my turn in is very late (it's easy to get drawn into the turn too early).
> I aim for the apex, 1 metre after the kerb on the right.
> I drive from the apex and aim to run parallel to the outside kerb on the last third.
> I stay 2 metres out from the first kerb on the right, through Hollywood, clip the second and overturn the bend, allowing a wide sweeping line through the next left at Craner Curves, apexing at the crown of the kerb.
> I drive hard from the apex and only use three-quarters of the track.
> I brake in a straight line parallel with the kerb on the left before I turn in at the last part of the kerb, on the left as I enter Old Hairpin.
> I apex on the crown of the kerb and drive hard, using all of the track on exit.
> I change my line to the right of the track for Starkeys, apex on the crown and drive hard.
> I look to the entrance of Schwantz and apex at the last third of the kerb on the curve, in preparation for McLeans, so that I can carry good corner speed here.
> I turn in and keep a metre off the kerb until the last third of the kerb where I apex.
> I accelerate hard, being aware of the camber dropping away.
> I clip the outside of the curve and run parallel with the edge of the track, up to Coppice.
> My turn in to Coppice is blind so my braking point is by judgement with the hedge/advertising sign on the inside.
> I take an early apex and run deep, being aware of the camber change.
> I let the bike flow to the outside of the track and accelerate progressively as the corner opens up.
> I aim for the apex, 1 metre after the second curb on the right, and clip the outside curb on the last quarter.
> I keep left as I go under the Dunlop Bridge and over the crest.

I move to the right side of the track, parallel to the curb as I enter the Fogarty Esses.
I turn in and take a late apex on the first curb, being careful not to carry too much speed and sacrifice my drive out.
I flick right and apex at the crown on the right, before accelerating hard, parallel with the last third of the curb on the outside.
I accelerate over the crest, being aware that there are few braking references into the next corner, so I use the barrier on the right and look for the curb as reference.
I keep tight to the curb, apex on the last third and accelerate out, parallel with the last third of the curb on the outside.
I accelerate over the crest towards Goddards.
Goddards is difficult to judge a braking marker, so I count 'one, two' as I go past my chosen reference point and start braking before I see the apex of the corner.
I apex on the last third, and as the camber pushes me into the bend I keep tight to the apex and drive hard over the start-finish line.

(C. Moore)

If you are as familiar with your chosen circuit as this racer is with Donington, I would like to think that you are able to picture every corner and every straight in your mind in just as much detail. Of course, not all of the information you need will be in the script. For example, the script above takes place on a dry track in good conditions. You should therefore have a 'wet track' imagery sequence as well as a 'drying track' sequence and, indeed, as many other variations as you think are necessary to cover all eventualities. Recall that my asking you about the texture of the carpet or walls earlier now equates to the texture or surface of the track at various points. The fast, flowing airfield circuit of Thruxton is widely described amongst racers as 'bumpy'. This is all very well, but successful racers

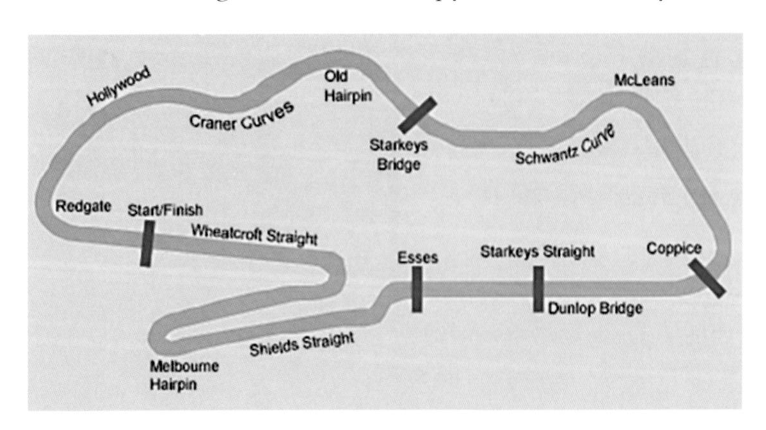

Donington Park GP Circuit. (Boot-Handford/Author)

will know exactly where the bumps are, how they will influence their bike or car, and what action is necessary to negotiate them.

Warning: the eight-minute lap

Having produced a script of the kind shown above, there is a real danger that it will be useless. If you talk yourself through the script word for word, you will be on for a lap of around eight minutes, whereas Donington should be lapped at around 1 minute 30 seconds or so, depending on what you are riding or driving. The script, however, is not useless. It should be used to get a grasp on the intricacies of the circuit and should become imprinted on your mind. You can then use it to formulate a simulated lap in real time. In order to do this you might modify your script in the way I have done below.

Accelerating from the apex of Goddard's, outside curb, last quarter, right of the track.
Left, left, left, Redgate.
Brake, turn in late.
Apex.
Gas Gas Gas.
Stay out. Clip curb. Wide sweep. Apex Crown.
Gas Gas Gas.
Brake, turn in. Old Hairpin.
Gas Gas Gas. All of the track on exit.
Move right for Starkeys, apex on crown. Gas Gas Gas.
Carry corner speed.
Turn in. Apex.
Gas Gas Gas.
Clip the outside of the curve, up to Coppice.
Brakes. Control judgement.
Early apex, run deep.
Outside. Progressive Gas Gas Gas as corner opens.
Apex. Clip the outside curb.
Keep left. Under Dunlop Bridge and over crest.
Move right.
Turn in, late apex.
Flick right and apex at the crown. Gas Gas Gas.
Gas Gas Gas. Brake.
Tight to the curb. Apex. Gas.
Gas over the crest towards Goddards.
Reference point. Brakes.
Apex. Camber. Tight Apex. Drive Hard. Lap done.

You can see how this script has been created from the previous one. It is not the words that make the script. Rather it is the visual imagery in your mind that brings the script to life. If these words don't allow you to 'see' the lap, then you need to adapt them until the lap is brought to life. Keep practising until it appears for you!

Set a stopwatch. Ride or drive the lap in your mind. There should be no difference between your mental lap time and your real lap time. This is an indicator of successful mental imagery.

A correctly designed mental imagery sequence can be used to rehearse even the finest of detail, to the point where it becomes second nature. As pointed out earlier, this should free-up available mental resources for strategy. The table below can be used as a template for writing an imagery script. It contains details for a motorcycle racer I have worked with in the past and acts as a mental rehearsal for the events leading up to the start of a race and the first corner. See if you can identify with it. The script can easily be adapted to suit any part of a race weekend or any form of motorsport.

Phase 1: Basic awareness	**Phase 2: Inclusion of details**		**Phase 3: Refinement of detail**
	Descriptors	**Actions and emotions**	
1 Preparing for race	Confident, excited, aware of crowd and cameras.	Feel full of energy, confident in my ability. I can hear the large crowd and the television crews.	I am preparing for the start of the race. I am feeling energised, confident and ready to race.
2 Into grid position	End of warm-up lap, look for grid position. Body position on grid. Hold bike.	I find my grid position and move purposefully into it. I see the crowd and feel alert and confident. I put my leg down and grip the handlebars.	I come around the last corner on the warm-up lap and move towards my grid position. I can see and hear the crowd as I position the bike purposefully. I position my left foot firmly on the floor and hold the bike. I relax my shoulders and then grip the handlebars purposefully.

3 Focus mentally	Focus on lights and turn 1. Deep breathe. Think of exploding into life when lights go out.	Focus on the lights and then on to the first corner. Picture my route into turn 1 as if I own it. Breathe deeply. Talk my way through start procedure. No awareness of competitors. Explode into life when lights go out. I feel relaxed and mentally ready.	I focus on the lights and beyond, to the first corner. I see a corridor open only to me. I breathe in deeply and am ready to explode into life as soon as the lights go out. The competitors around me do not exist: it is just myself against the track.
4 Prepare for lights	After the warning, I get my body into position, in readiness for lights.	After the warning, I get my legs comfortably into position, followed by my arms, in readiness for the lights. My left and right hands are busy holding clutch or throttle. I feel my heart rate increasing but this inspires confidence: this is my adrenaline kicking in.	I hear the warning for pit crew to clear the grid. I flex my leg as I hold the bike upright, ankle and knee slightly bent. I grip the left handlebar and hold the clutch lever in with one finger. I blip the throttle and rev the engine repetitively as I grip the right handlebar gently. My body weight is far forward and my heart rate increases.

5 Lights out: drive	Lights go out. I fire off the line smoothly and successfully.	The lights go out and I get the bike moving smoothly, yet quickly, my hands working in harmony to produce a good start. I feel a burst of explosive energy as my adrenaline seemingly provides a shot of nitrous oxide to my mental engine.	The lights go out and my clutch finger smoothly releases the clutch as my throttle hand opens smoothly. My left leg tucks in behind the fairing and I push my weight forward to keep the weight over the front wheel.
6 Approach turn 1	Good body position, relaxed. Excellent acceleration and pace.	My body is perfectly poised on the bike. I am relaxed, yet focused. I aim for the corridor opening up in my mind and fire into it smoothly and incredibly quickly. The acceleration makes me feel energised, powerful and unstoppable.	I am getting drive towards turn 1 and am firing down my mental corridor. No one can touch me and the racing line is mine: I own it. I have already overtaken three people because I have an empty corridor to ride into. My acceleration is sublime and I reach turn 1 exactly as planned. While others are still fighting, I am looking ahead and planning for turn 2 …

Practising imagery before the event

Mental practice is essential. After deciding on whether to use internal or external imagery, you should consider another aspect of imagery, related to the job that you want it to help you with. You need to decide whether your imagery needs to be a general or specific sequence. Then you need to decide whether you need it for cognitive or motivational reasons. If it is to do with race strategy, it will be cognitive. If it is to do with boosting confidence, for example, it will be motivational. The table below will help you in deciding which type of mental imagery you may need:

	Cognitive	Motivational
General	Strategic planning *eg* imaging a strategy to overtake number 3 on the brakes into Coppice.	Arousal *eg* imaging increases or decreases in your heart rate before the five-minute call.
Specific	Skills-practice *eg* imaging the fine balance between throttle and brake through the chicane.	Goal-response *eg* imaging standing on the podium after a successful race.

Adapted from Paivio (1985)

Having decided which imagery to use, you are now ready to practise. This is where we must return to the issue of controlling the mental imagery sequence. I would ask you to return to the living room scenario discussed earlier, but this time to imagine a friend or colleague sitting on one of the chairs. I would then make suggestions about that person. Are they smiling? Drinking a cup of coffee? How are they sitting? – and so on. Next, I would ask you to imagine the person getting up and switching the television on to watch the motorsport. You should be able to control what is happening within the imagery sequence. In developing control, it is then necessary, for example, for you to imagine an anxiety-evoking situation from your racing. This might be the moments leading up to being called out for a qualifying session. Perhaps you may focus on the feelings of anxiety – tension in the shoulders and neck; increased heart rate; dry mouth; clammy hands. I would then take each of these and ask you to imagine your shoulders and neck becoming more relaxed, the speed of your heartbeat reducing, saliva beginning to return in your mouth, and the perspiration on your hands beginning to dry. If you have been able to focus on these things returning to normal, *you* have controlled all the things causing heightened anxiety and you are now ready to focus on the qualifying session. The power of verbalising the situation will prepare you for the event when it happens in reality. As I have pointed out throughout this chapter, the key word, of course, is *practise*.

Combining imagery with performance data

I worked with one competitor who used his mental imagery skills in an innovative way. We sat down and worked through his activities during free practice and qualifying sessions. At every session, data was collected about his times and speed through each sector of the circuit and used to find the best settings for the particular circuit. I suggested that he used adapted versions of his mental imagery sequence to practise going faster through those sectors in his mind where the data was showing that he was slower than other competitors. So while technicians worked on suspension settings, the racer went off to work on his mental imagery sequences. As one would expect, during the next session his efforts were repaid with faster sector times, faster lap times and a better grid position for the race.

Practising imagery after the event

Although this seems rather strange, practising imagery sequences after an event is a useful technique. It can act as a kind of debrief to ensure that the imagery used before the event was appropriate. If you find that certain things were missing or were different to your sequence, then now is the time to incorporate this new information before it gets forgotten. This will enhance your store of information about this particular circuit for next year. It is worth pointing out that you must remain updated on changes to circuits over the close season. There would be nothing worse on the first sighting lap next year than expecting to exit the penultimate corner only to find that someone has suddenly built a chicane into the track! I have in mind here the relatively recent inclusion of the chicane before the start-finish straight at Silverstone – a much-disliked modification that F1 drivers have the luxury of not having to negotiate.

Imagery aids

Competitors may find that various aids will help them to develop and enhance their mental imagery sequences. I will briefly highlight some of these here.

Practising mental imagery may lead to improved sector and lap times. (sutton-images.com)

Imagery scripts

Having developed your first written imagery script, you might now be considering variations of it designed to cover different situations at the same circuit – you will recall me mentioning the usefulness of different scripts for varying weather conditions. You will begin to build up an actual set of electronic or paper copies of your sequences. Keep them together in a file for reference purposes, and in case you need to return to them to refresh your memory. Think of this file as being a recipe book of circuits.

Videotape/DVD

You may find that the imagery sequences you now possess are adequate but need enhancing. It may be that videotapes or DVDs will help you – *eg* F1 season reviews, WSB season reviews for World Superbikes, or BTCC season reviews for British Touring Cars. It is far easier to watch something on videotape or DVD when you know what you are looking for, so ask yourself which elements you think may be missing from your imagery sequence. Use the videotape or DVD to hunt for that information. Of course, there is no reason why you cannot also obtain personal video footage of yourself by camcorder. Some teams use photographic evidence to show drivers or riders how they are negotiating particular sections of the circuit. Such pictures are available from specialist motorsport photographers at major events (*eg* jakobebry.co.uk). Alternatively, a video sequence in real time would be helpful.

Computer games

As I mentioned earlier, computer gaming software is now so good that it can provide a developing racer with circuit information without having to go to the circuit. Whilst bearing in mind the warning about changes to circuits, computer games can provide some information about the sequence of corners and straights. Remember that it rarely if ever provides information about gradients and camber, so you will need to add these to your sequence following a test day or practice session.

Audio record

Some competitors prefer to convert their imagery scripts into CD or MP3 format. This, of course, is perfectly acceptable. Indeed, if you are able to obtain video footage from a race at the particular circuit, perhaps from last season, you might add your verbalised script as a voice-over. However, I would warn against becoming heavily reliant on a CD or MP3, simply because if you happen to leave it at home by accident, or the batteries run out on your MP3 player, you might panic! Audio records are potentially useful to get you started, but once you are familiar with the imagery sequence it should be stored in your mind for ease of reference when needed (recall what I said at the start of this chapter about strengthening connections in the human brain).

Contextual setting

Wherever possible you should aim to carry out your mental imagery sequence in a contextually appropriate setting, such as the pits, paddock or your motorhome at the circuit while other races are taking place etc. This will provide an element of reality.

Research in psychology reveals that recall from memory works well if it takes place in the same environment in which it was learned. The same applies to the emotional state that you are in when you learn. If you are relaxed when you learn, you will remember more if you are relaxed when tested; but if you are tense, you will not be able to remember as much. I flippantly tell my students that if they revise for an examination when they are drunk, the theory suggests that they should remember more if they are drunk during the examination. Of course, I swiftly move on to point out the obvious flaw in this argument! In psychology there are always exceptions to the rule.

Contextual props

If you are unable to carry out your mental imagery sequence at the circuit, perhaps because you are developing it before you even get there, then there are things that you can do to enhance the sequence. As children, many of us played with toy steering wheels and pretended our bicycles were motorcycles. The use of contextual props works along similar lines. When using mental imagery sequences at home or away from the circuit, get into your racing clothing, put your helmet on, and if you can sit on your race bike or in your racing car, all the better, although this is not essential. Now run through the mental imagery sequence in your mind. I'm sure you will agree that it feels so much more real than yesterday, when you only had your casual clothes on. I could list any number of contextual props here, but I would rather you consider what is significant for your own script. As always, think of the finest of detail, even down to the type of drinking bottle that you use. If you would take a drink in reality just before exiting the pit lane, then fill your bottle before carrying out the sequence and pick it up for real, at the point in your sequence that is appropriate.

Summary

In this chapter I have discussed what mental imagery is, possible theories underlying it, and its use in different situations and for different reasons. I have gone on to explain how to set up a bank of imagery sequences and suggested ways of practising and refining these. I would suggest that you practise each element of imagery (general; specific; cognitive; motivational) so that you can master each of them. You never know when a new challenge will emerge, and if practise in one element is lacking it always seems to be in the one that is needed right now. Of course, it takes time to develop imagery sequences that work but I would argue that the time devoted to such practice will pay dividends in the long run.

Chapter 12

Mental toughness

Introduction

Mental toughness is about overcoming anxiety and fear in competitive situations. It is about the will to go that extra mile, the ability to push when everyone else is flagging, and to endure pain and hardship in an attempt to achieve a goal. A general definition which helps to identify key elements of mental toughness is 'the ability to stand tall in the face of adversity ... a psychic resiliency that allows you to rebound from setbacks and failures time and time again' (Loehr, 1995, p.11). You can accept poor performance as a failing in yourself and your skill or as a test of your capability.

So, mental toughness is about endurance and stamina. It is completely psychological. It exists only in the head of the competitor. Mental toughness for one person will not necessarily be the same as mental toughness for another. It is therefore unique to each individual. This is why competitors can lose a race before they have even started. If you have been psyched out by an opponent before you even leave the start line, you will suffer the consequences of lacking in mental toughness. So, all you need to do is read this chapter and you will have all the answers on how to become mentally tough, yes? Well, no! In this chapter I will provide guidance on aspects of psychological functioning that may help you to highlight what mental toughness means to you. I will refer constantly to many of the other chapters and show you that mental toughness is more of a culmination of elements, rather like the pieces in a jigsaw puzzle that should help to create the overall picture that is mental toughness.

If there were to be a single piece of the jigsaw that is bigger than any other, I would perhaps argue that it is self-confidence. Without self-confidence it is virtually impossible to develop or maintain mental toughness. Surely, then, the simple answer is to read the chapter on self-confidence to solve the problem? Well, no! Self-confidence may be the largest piece in the jigsaw, but it is itself made up of many smaller pieces. Which brings us back to square one. The key to issues of mental toughness and self-confidence lies in reading this book, identifying areas to work on and developing steadily over time.

In order to acquire mental toughness it will be necessary to work through any of the factors that you believe are missing from your 'mental DNA'. I like this idea of using mental DNA as an analogy, suggesting that toughness is made up of component parts and all we need to do is obtain these, assemble them and then incorporate them into our genetic make-up. Of course, I am not suggesting that we can change our genetic code. But I do have an image in my mind of creating a psychological profile that is adapted to survive. This fits nicely with Darwin's idea of survival of the fittest. As Dakar Rally racers are only too aware, when you have to endure dune after dune for many miles, stamina and survival are the only things that should be on your mind.

In working through the chapters in this book, you will be getting closer and closer to assembling all of the ingredients necessary for you to be psychologically strong when everyone else is beginning to flag. If you are confident that you have a wide range of skills and techniques to help you through any challenge, you will be more likely to move into 'the zone' for racing, that different level of consciousness where everything seems effortless. I will lead on to this later in the next chapter, when I talk about flow states.

The initial question is therefore how do you know what the component parts are and whether you possess them or not? One way of finding out is by using the technique of performance profiling, which I have used many times with racers to great effect.

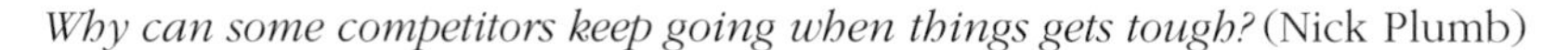

Why can some competitors keep going when things gets tough? (Nick Plumb)

Performance profiling

A simple yet effective method of identifying missing elements in your mental DNA is through the use of performance profiling. Performance profiling was developed by Butler and Hardy in 1992 and can be used to discover a competitor's perception of his or her physical, technical and psychological abilities at the present time. Completing the performance profile is a three-step process. Firstly, you should think of a person in your discipline who you would aspire to emulate. There is no right or wrong answer here. It does not have to be someone at the very top of their game, such as Räikkönen, Hamilton or Rossi, although it often is a person of this calibre. It does not have to be somebody still competing or indeed still alive: Michael Schumacher, John Surtees, Barry Sheene, Ayrton Senna or Juan Manuel Fangio are all equally appropriate. Even somebody in your current race series would be appropriate if you believe they have qualities that are helping them to succeed. Having identified a role model, the second step is to write down a list of qualities that you think this competitor has or had that made them so special. It is also important to write down what you mean by these qualities, since you may not remember exactly what you meant if you look back a few months later. The accompanying response sheet will provide a template to help you do this.

To give some examples, perhaps you think that stamina is an important characteristic of the competitor you wish to emulate. The meaning of 'stamina' for you might be the ability to stay out on track during the rain on a test session when most other people have pitted. Alternatively, it might be the ability to push

Who do you admire most in motorsport? (LAT)

harder despite an injury. So the definition can change even if the word stays the same. Another of your role model's qualities might perhaps be concentration, which might be represented by their ability to regain focus after a racing incident, or to retain a high level of attention for a whole race weekend. There is no right or wrong definition of any of these characteristics, which depend entirely on how you perceive them.

Having written the meanings in column two of your record sheet, it is then necessary to complete the final two columns. In column three you need to rate, out of ten, how highly you think each particular quality is represented in the competitor you admire. You must then rate yourself in the same way, putting your own perceived score in the fourth column. You will then have two figures, let's say for stamina: perhaps you rate your 'ideal person' as 9 and yourself as 4 at this moment in time. This provides information on where you want or need to be in terms of stamina and where you are now. All (and I use the word loosely) you need to do now is find a way of attaining a rating of 9. The performance profile has therefore highlighted a goal to be pursued. The chapter on goal setting provides detailed guidance on how to achieve this goal.

Performance profiling record sheet

Think about a racer whom you admire (past or present) and consider the qualities that racer possesses/possessed that enables/enabled them to produce the performances you admire.

It may help to split these into separate categories:

- physical
- technical
- tactical/psychological

Write these qualities, together with a brief definition of what you mean by that quality. Do not complete columns 3 or 4 at this stage. There are no right or wrong answers: only what you think is important.

Quality	**Meaning**	**Rating (0–10)** IDEAL	**Rating (0–10)** YOU
eg concentration	*eg* the ability to stay focused after being 'nudged' in the previous session on track	*eg* 9	*eg* 3

Now that you have completed columns 1 and 2, please rate your ideal racer on each of these qualities (column 3) and then rate yourself at this moment in time on the same qualities (column 4).

The scale is from 0 to 10, where 0 = a feeling that you do not possess that quality at all, and 10 = a feeling that you are very strong in that quality.

Adapted from Butler and Hardy (1992)

Interpreting the performance profile

As you can see from the record sheet, the racer is guided towards splitting the required qualities into three separate categories: physical; technical; and tactical/psychological. I recommend that you do this for two reasons. Firstly, it provides some clues as to what is required. Many people struggle with the performance profile if they are not given some help in starting to complete the record sheet. Of course, there is a fine balance to be reached between making suggestions to the racer on the one hand and putting words in their mouth on the other. The performance profile is self-focused (it is your own opinion of what is needed to be successful in racing), and as such, completing it should be a self-focused activity (it should be about you). By providing three possible categories, these categories provide a foundation upon which to build and, therefore, guide you in making a start.

It goes without saying that a sport psychologist is expecting to see a list of psychological qualities with which they can work. Although this is obviously where they are looking to provide support and guidance, it is only half of the story. I am not an expert in physical or technical aspects of many sports. Nevertheless, I believe that it is important to focus on more than just the psychological elements underlying possible 'weaknesses'. When I interpret performance profiles, I look to the psychological factors but also pay attention to those technical and physical qualities appearing on the record sheet. It may be that a theme emerges. A solution regarding self-confidence may lie in suggesting a change of weekly training routine in the fitness centre. Of course, I would need to make it clear that the racer communicates this to their personal trainer, who is more qualified than I am to provide this particular support. I might implement a goal-setting programme around gym-work that helps to build stamina and strength, and this has a knock-on effect on the racer's confidence. There may be more factors that are indicating a particular theme and the rule of thumb is that the more factors that emerge, the greater the likelihood that the problem can be confirmed. This helps everyone concerned from being sidetracked or taking an inappropriate course of action, only to discover that the problem is still present. The message, therefore, is carefully to consider possible interrelationships between the qualities that you write down, and keep an open mind when interpreting the performance profile. It is there to help you, not to throw weaknesses at you.

The example quality that I listed on the record sheet, 'concentration', is purely for illustrative purposes. Equally, the meaning I have provided may be personal to me – which is why it is important, if you write down the same quality, for you to clarify its meaning. Two racers might both consider concentration to be important to their racing, but might think of it in entirely different terms. For racer number one, concentration could be as I have described it, 'the ability to stay focused after being nudged during the previous session on track', whereas for racer number two it could be 'thinking about strategy'. Here we have two completely different interpretations. The advice and guidance that I might give to racer number one would be useless for racer number two and vice versa. For racer number one, I would perhaps investigate the reasons why concentration is lost after being hit on track. One might think that this would be obvious, but sport psychologists do not jump to conclusions. A different racer might not be distracted by being hit and may instead perceive it simply as a challenge in jostling for position. Yet for racer number one, it appears to be causing a major distraction.

With racer number two I might perhaps explore his or her activities before leaving the pit garage to establish whether a pre-performance routine is being used. I could also explore whether concentration is lost before he or she gets on the bike or into the car, or whether it only happens in the few hours leading up to the race, or before a qualifying session. Having identified the source of the problem, a solution can be suggested through one or more of the techniques outlined in the practical chapters. So, the same word, concentration, does not necessarily mean that the same problem is being experienced or that the same solution will be successful.

Once you have completed the record sheet you have the necessary information to make informed decisions on a potential course of action. Although the traditional method of recording the information in a diagrammatic way is by

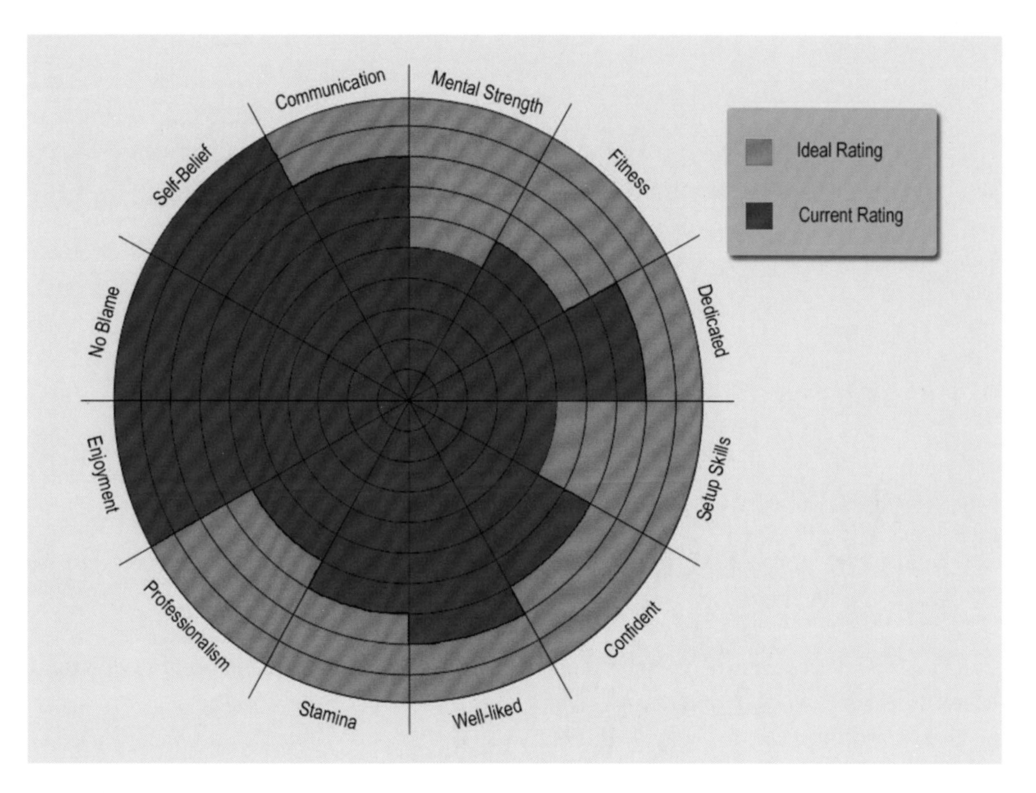

A 'traditional' summary of a performance profile, showing a competitor's initial ratings. (Boot-Handford/Author)

An electronically-generated summary of a performance profile, showing a competitor's initial ratings against those of his ideal motorsport icon. (Boot-Handford/Author)

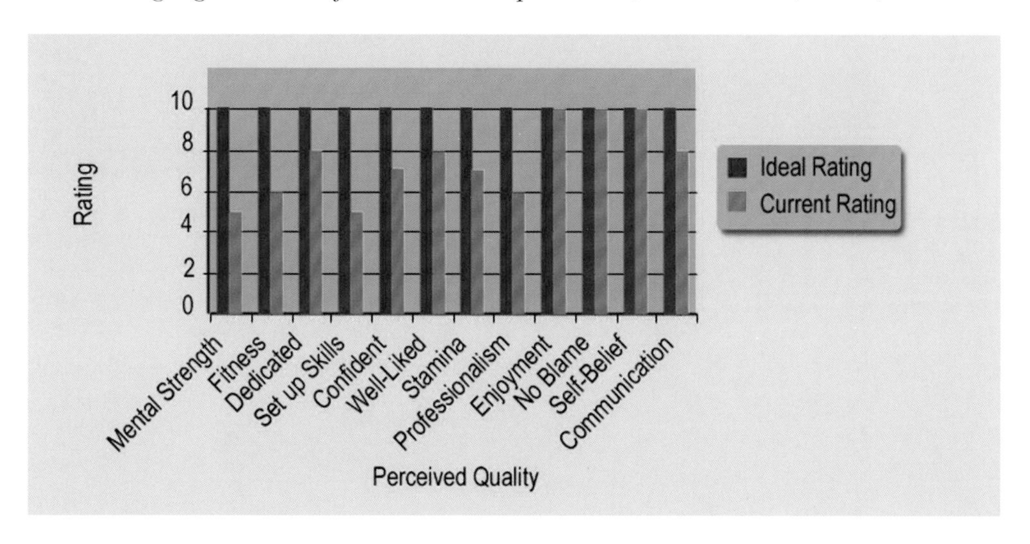

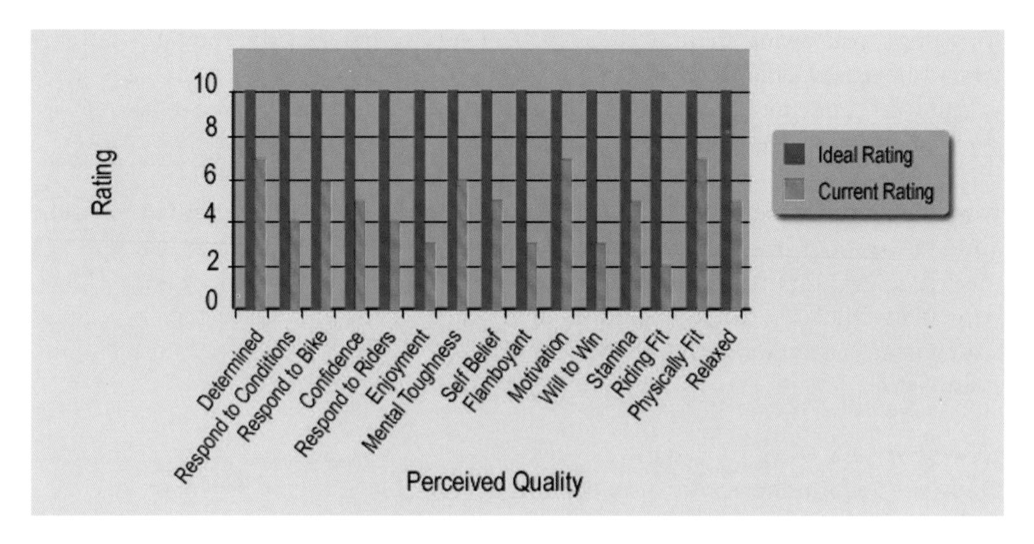

An example performance profile highlighting lower perceived scores.
(Boot-Handford/Author)

transferring it to a circular chart, my colleague Julia West at the University of Worcester has developed a computer-generated Excel spreadsheet for the performance profile. In this way data can be stored electronically for use as required. More importantly, it provides a quick method of obtaining a visual representation of where your perception of your racing qualities stand in relation

An electronically-generated summary of a performance profile, showing a competitor's improved ratings over time compared to his initial ratings of himself.
(Boot-Handford/Author)

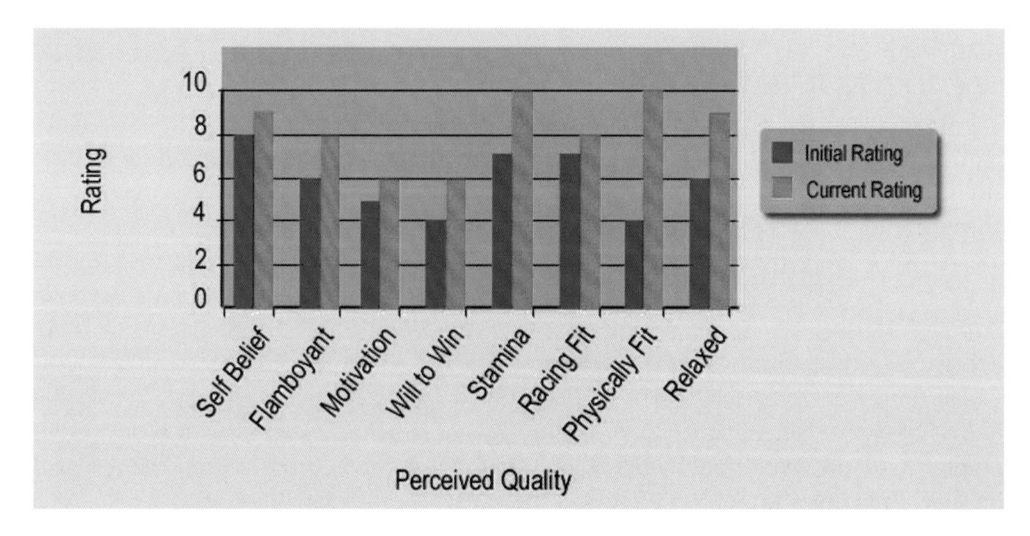

to where you want them to be. You need to transfer the ratings into the spreadsheet and obtain a computer-generated bar chart. I also usually ask racers to print this and put a copy somewhere where they can see it on a regular basis, such as on the fridge door.

The performance profile, therefore, serves as a constant reminder of areas to work on and complements goal setting wonderfully. You can access it at any time and complete an up-to-date version as and when you choose to, so that you can see whether progress in one area has led to improvements in others. This is particularly the case for confidence. If you set out to work on other aspects of your racing, I guarantee that these will affect your confidence levels, usually in a positive way.

Low scores: a word of warning

Once the record sheet and profile have been produced, it is important that you deflect attention away from the negative points in favour of the positive ones. It is easy for a racer to see the low scores and interpret them as a sign of failure. This, of course, is not the reality of the situation. Rather, I tend to suggest to racers that this provides them with an opportunity to see marked improvements on these scores over a period of time, a point that I will deal with shortly. Low scores may therefore be seen in a positive way. Improvements should raise self-esteem and self-confidence, and, thus, performance.

Strengths and challenges: a word of warning

The initial focus after interpreting the performance profile may be to prioritise some of the qualities where you need to make progress. I would always advise against focusing on too many of these at one time, since to do so may have detrimental effects that could damage the practitioner-racer relationship. So I tend to recommend writing down three strengths and three weaknesses. I would here swiftly reiterate the point I make elsewhere in this book, that 'weaknesses' should be re-branded as 'challenges'.

I must, however, offer a word of warning. As I have said elsewhere, it is human nature not to look at oneself for faults but rather to blame others for failings. A similar principle can be applied to performance profiling. I have heard the comment many times, 'I will work on these three strengths to get them from a 7 to a 9 or 10.' Every time this comment is made to me, what I actually hear in my head is, 'I would rather stick my head in the sand and pretend the problem isn't there!' In other words, it is far easier to work on things that one is already accomplished at, than to take on the hard work of improving things that one is not so good at. So when the three challenges are listed it is important for you to focus on and discuss ways in which progress can be made. It is actually quite common to discover that by working on the low scores the higher scores also improve, having a knock-on effect on the racer's performance overall.

Performance profiles over a period of time

I mentioned earlier the possibility of using electronic versions of performance profiling. The main benefit of doing so is that you can then compare performance profiles over a period of time. It is not sufficient to produce one performance profile. The first one that you produce should be used as a starting point, a baseline measure. It is the one against which future performance profiles are compared. Otherwise, what is the point of the task? The performance profile on page 178 shows huge improvements in many areas, and those where ratings have remained almost the same may not be cause for concern.

The frequency with which you should complete a performance profile will depend on certain things. One of these is the urgency of showing progress in overcoming a problem. If you keep crashing and are losing self-confidence, it is important to focus on this aspect of the profile in order to keep confidence levels as high as possible. Organising test sessions on track to work on communicating

Are you tough enough for the challenges facing you? (Volkswagen UK)

set-up differences may address the issue of crashing and this should have a complementary effect on self-confidence. A second consideration should be availability of time. Racers are increasingly busy during periods away from the circuit. Sponsors require the racer to appear at publicity events, the media are keen to conduct interviews, and supporters are constantly looking for opportunities to meet their heroes. Time is, therefore, a precious commodity. Completing a performance profile on a regular basis adds to the activities on a racer's agenda. However, it is important that you allocate an appropriate amount of time to mental training.

In answering the question, 'How often should I complete a performance profile?' I would recommend at sufficiently long intervals to see a difference, but not so long that motivation to make progress diminishes. This answer is of little use at one level, but it illustrates the fact that racers are individuals, and consequently I cannot be more specific than saying you should complete a performance profile regularly. This may be at four-month intervals, after every three races, or even between single races. Personal preference plays a role here. A racer may, under guidance, select the window of opportunity when completing a performance profile will be most effective.

I am working with racers this season who complete a performance profile twice during the race weekend, once during free practice and then an hour or so before the race. The team manager, senior race engineers, racers and I have a pre-race briefing. The performance profile covers psychological and well as machine performance. So we may evaluate confidence levels in relation to front-end tyre grip or suspension settings. This innovative way of using the performance profile to incorporate race settings enables the race engineers to assess their own interpretation of riders' needs, which feeds back into rider confidence, which, in turn minimises anxiety.

Performance profiling: why so late in the book?

If performance profiling is so important in providing beneficial information on a racer's current profile, you might wonder why it appears so late in the book. This is completely intentional. There is little point in asking you to evaluate your current psychological profile if you are unaware of the kind of things that may be influencing it. In face-to-face circumstances, a sport psychologist has the luxury of being able to discuss issues with the racer and explore elements of the racer's psyche. It is not possible to do this in a book. Instead it is the information contained in the book that must guide you in questioning yourself effectively. Having gained knowledge from the preceding chapters, you are now in an informed position to begin to think about your own profile and the kind of elements in your armoury that require development. This applies whether you are reading the book as a novice at the very beginning of your motorsport career or as a competent racer with many years of experience behind you.

Performance profiling can be used for all sorts of things. If necessary, I could have completed my own performance profile before embarking on this book. I could have considered the qualities required to complete the project, my strengths and challenges, my skills and areas where I lack expertise, before setting goals to develop my profile into that of a successful author. If you think outside of the box you can use performance profiling to your advantage. In terms of mental toughness, however, performance profiling only serves as a starting point and does not provide all the information you might require, and you will need to complement it with some questionnaire data. It is to this that I will now turn.

Mental Toughness Questionnaires

If you want to collect personal information to see how strong you might be mentally for next year's Suzuka 8-hour, Le Mans du 24 heures, or the excruciating Dakar Rally, then you have to go down the route of exploring mental toughness.

Various questionnaires for measuring mental toughness exist. The questions below are derived from the *Mental Toughness Test* (Loehr, 1982). In order not to bias a racer's responses, I would usually ask them to complete a mental toughness questionnaire, in conjunction with a performance profile, before debriefing them. You might like to complete the questions below before reading on.

Do I see myself as more of a winner than a loser in competition?
Do I believe in myself as a racer?
Do I remain confident when the race isn't going my way?
Can I perform toward the upper range of my talent and skill?

If you have answered 'yes' your self-confidence may be high.

Am I highly motivated to motivate myself and do my best?
Do I set goals to keep me working hard as a racer?
Am I prepared to give whatever it takes to reach my full potential as a racer?
Do I wake up in the morning excited about training and racing?

If you have answered 'yes' your motivation may be high.

Am I able to keep my focus during competition?
Does my mind remain calm during critical moments of a race?
Am I able to clear interfering emotions quickly and regain my focus?
Am I able to focus on successful lines and technique as I race?

If you have answered 'yes' your attentional control may be high.

Am I able to think positively during competition?
Do I give 100 % effort during a race, no matter what?
Am I able to change negative moods into positive ones by controlling my thinking?
Can I turn 'crisis' into 'opportunity'?

If you have answered 'yes' your ability to control your attitude may be high.

Am I able to keep strong positive emotion flowing during competition?
Do I enjoy competition even when I face lots of difficult problems?
Do I get inspired for the challenge in tough situations?
Does racing give me a genuine sense of joy and fulfilment?

If you have answered 'yes' your 'positive energy' may be high.

Am I able to visualise myself racing successfully?
Am I able to mentally rehearse my technical racing skills?
Do I visualise working through challenging situations prior to a race?
Do I use imagery before leaving the pits to me perform better?

If you have answered 'yes' your ability to control mental imagery may be high.

Do I get angry and frustrated during competition?
Do I get nervous or afraid in competition?
Do mistakes get me feeling and thinking negatively?
Do my muscles become overly tight during competition?

If you have answered '**NO**' your ability to minimise 'negative energy' may be high (low negative energy is a good thing!).

These sections may be the 'ingredients' of mental toughness. If you have all of the right ingredients, there is a strong likelihood that you will be a successful racer. If you don't have these ingredients, you can obtain them with the help of this book and guidance from a sport psychologist with suitable experience in motorsport.

Interpreting Mental Toughness Questionnaires

For sport psychologists, interpreting mental toughness questionnaires is quite straightforward. The skill lies in reaching a solution based on the information obtained. The questions above and performance profile aim to draw out the type of information covered by the preceding chapters of this book and show that mental toughness is a combination of many separate, yet inter-related elements.

When a sport psychologist and racer sit down to discuss the information provided by the performance profile and the mental toughness questionnaire, certain themes usually emerge. The sport psychologist can then begin to observe emerging patterns and can establish a strong profile of the racer. If the two types of information-gathering do not concur with each other, this does not mean that discrepancies exist, but merely that the 'issues' may be less pronounced and in need of further exploration. Let's face it, the human mind is extremely complicated and the 'quick fix' is rarely a panacea for all 'ills'.

Practical techniques to improve mental toughness

I run sessions on mental toughness at the University of Worcester and usually ask competitors to tell me how they normally react to various adverse situations, for example:

- Following a cycle of inconsistent performance.
- Following a spate of distracted incidences involving poor decision making.
- After competing against more experienced opposition, perhaps as a wild card entry in an international race.
- After a DNF for the third consecutive time.
- After crashing and receiving a minor injury.
- After crashing and receiving a major injury.

The key to mental toughness is 'positive optimism'

Positive optimism is about thinking in positive terms and seeing problems as challenges. Positive optimism can be achieved by:

- Becoming aware of yourself and your body.
- Knowing the ideal performance state and being able to adjust this when necessary.
- Controlling/channelling thoughts and feelings.

I favour three techniques that will help you to achieve positive optimism and enhance mental toughness. These are listed below. You will see how important they are when you work through the practical example (which uses mental imagery from Chapter 11) below.

Disciplined positive thinking

You should practise positive thinking and positive imagery with the underlying pretext that ill-disciplined negative thinking leads to ill-disciplined negative performance. This will also undermine your attempts to think positively. Think along the lines of forming a habit of positive thinking and imagery.

How would you react after crashing heavily? (Centurion Racing)

Prioritising positive and negative self-talk
You should be aware of and accept that negative thoughts and feelings sometimes occur when there is a challenge to be met (a sort of 'no pain, no gain' philosophy). You should explore the challenge and identify whether this is something which can be solved immediately or which should be sidelined until a more appropriate moment.

Controlling and channelling thoughts and feelings
You should familiarise yourself with continually identifying and attempting to change negative thoughts and feelings to positive ones. Sometimes humour can help to immediately relieve a stressful situation. Think about a situation that you thought was funny because you made a simple basic mistake. As soon as you make light of it, it becomes less intense and you will feel better. Alternatively, if you have made a serious error of judgement try to find the humour in it somewhere. You will minimise its impact just by trivialising it. Of course, I am not suggesting that you don't look at the underlying problem – just don't do it at this

moment in time when you need to channel your thoughts and feelings into getting on with the challenge. Thinking energetically also transfers to performance in a positive way. Practise thinking quickly and making quick confident decisions without changing your mind, then quickly evaluate your progress so that the positive thoughts and successful ongoing performance will reinforce the fact that you are doing the job.

An example 'energising' mental imagery script

Read through the following script, following each step at a time. As is usual with mental imagery scripts, some people find that they can't stop laughing at first because the wording sounds so ridiculously funny. This is quite normal. If this happens to you, simply try to follow the instructions by concentrating a little harder. You will get into the rhythm fairly quickly and will then reap the benefits.

Step	Instruction
1	Find a quiet environment where you can make yourself comfortable.
2	Close your eyes and allow yourself to focus on your breathing.
3	When you feel focused and calm transfer your thoughts to your abdomen.
4	Imagine a ball of pure energy in your abdomen, which can move around your body when you control it.
5	As the energy ball travels down and then up your right leg it leaves behind a trace of pure energy that your muscles can use.
6	This energy ball then travels slowly down and up your left leg then back to your abdomen.
7	The energy ball then travels up and down your arms one at a time and back to your abdomen.
8	After energising your limbs, all your thoughts should focus on your powerful and precise movements.
9	Break off a piece of this energy ball and send it up towards your head.
10	When it reaches your brain, all your thoughts become sharp and focused, and your decisions become quick and precise.
11	Bring yourself back to the present, by counting from 10 down to 1, and remind yourself how you feel refreshed, full of energy and mentally strong enough to take on any challenge that the race throws at you.

Adapted from West (2005)

If you are unsure when to use a script of this type, I would suggest that sitting on the starting grid, focusing on the first corner, would be an ideal time to experience the 'energy ball' flowing around your body mentally. As the lights go out the energy explodes and you burst into action, first into the corner and mentally strong.

Self-belief is important if you are to maintain mental toughness. (LAT)

You may need to 're-energise' during the race. Let's imagine that you are beginning to drop off the pace at two-thirds distance. What better time to use the 'energy ball' tactic, providing you with an instant burst of pace? With practice even just thinking about the 'energy ball' will be enough, because you will have trained your brain to associate the mental image with mental strength. I often use this technique when cycling hard up hills (a hill cannot exist if I have enough mental strength to take whatever challenge the ride throws at me!).

A final comment

Having acquired various pieces of the jigsaw, you can, following the guidance offered in the preceding chapters, concentrate on putting those pieces together to form a complete picture. This may take some time or it may happen very quickly. When it happens is of no particular significance – what is more important is that it *does* happen.

Chapter 13

The chequered flag: concluding remarks

THE TITLE OF THIS IS CHAPTER suggests that having read the previous chapters, a racer is now completely equipped to be the best and the fastest and to take the chequered flag in first place at will. Of course, this is not the reality of the situation. This is only the beginning of the journey. I have provided you with the necessary 'tools of the trade' with which to do the job, but when we use any tools for the first time we tend to be rather ham-fisted until we understand that there is a certain technique to using them successfully. Psychological skills are no different. This chapter therefore provides guidance on developing these skills to the point where they can be used successfully time and time again, and suggests a way forward on the road to psychological success.

Persevere: Rome wasn't built in a day

I would never advocate trying to utilise any of the techniques or advice in this book without practising beforehand. There is little point in trying a new technique for the first time on race day, when the stakes are high. I would recommend practising techniques away from the race circuit, or during test days. Having done so, it is then necessary to implement them during free practice before progressing to qualifying and then race days. I have heard the comment on many occasions, 'Well I tried it for a lap or two and it didn't work.' My response is usually something along the lines of, 'Well, do you think you gave it sufficient time to work?' There are also days when it seems impossible to find the correct set-up for your car or bike, yet we persevere.

Go slower in order to go faster?

It is essential for you to be aware that there will possibly be a dip in performance before an improvement occurs. A racer needs to get used to the way a new piece of equipment changes their racing, and if you acquire a new psychological skill the case is no different. While you are developing these skills you may go slower on track initially, but with practice you will begin to improve and your performance will go beyond its previous level. So be prepared to go slower before going faster. Of course, this will not always be the case. On many occasions a psychological skill can have an immediate, positive effect on performance. The message is simple. You must practise your psychological skills well in advance of the time that you need them most!

Staleness: reaching a rut or a plateau?

There will be times when you reach a plateau beyond which you just cannot seem to go. Again, this is a common situation in which to find yourself and is not a problem. Indeed, acknowledging that you have reached a plateau or rut is vital to progress. Too many racers avoid looking at themselves when progress is not being made. Reading this book should have enabled you to be open and honest with yourself, so acknowledge the rut and begin searching for a solution. This may involve, for example, changing aspects of your racing style, pre-performance routine, concentration strategy or relaxation routine.

A rut is a hole. If you view the situation as a rut, then negative psychological connotations will take hold. You can fall into a rut or hole and would have to

Refocus your thoughts so that a 'rut' becomes a 'plateau' with a new set of challenges.
(David.WillowPhotography.co.uk)

climb out of it, a difficult thing to do perhaps. On the other hand, a plateau is a plain. It implies that you have embarked on a climb and reached a wide expanse of land with various directions in which to proceed. If you view the situation as a plateau the problem presents itself more as a choice: 'Which direction shall I go in and what resources will I need to reach my destination?' Suddenly you have opportunities rather than difficulties, and you need to evaluate your options in order to decide which direction to head off in.

The rut/plateau metaphor works nicely in motorsport. I have spoken to many racers who, when faced with a rut, try harder and harder to overcome the problem and end up making the situation worse because they are trying too hard. My advice would be to take a step back, assess the situation, use the techniques offered in this book, and ask the 'How' question: 'How do I ...?' You are then looking for solutions rather than barriers.

Rewards

I mentioned rewards in the chapter on goal setting. It is important for racers to reward themselves when things are going well. It is equally important to do this when things are not going so well. This is perhaps a strange thing to say, but in fact it is not as strange as it appears. The key lies in the type of reward. If you are struggling, then you need to look for the smallest of improvements or positive elements in your racing. If you made the wrong tyre choice and came in last in the race, but stayed on track when you were on slicks and everyone else was on wets, then you should reward yourself with a few words of congratulation for doing a good job in the face of adversity. Always look for the positive elements and give yourself a pat on the back. Beware of rewards that may take your focus away. If you focus on winning the prize money or a promotional car, for example, your focus is taken away from the job of racing. Focus on the job and the rewards will come as by-products. Focus on the prizes and you will lose the race *and* the prize!

Commitment

Commitment is vital if you are to be, or remain, successful. If you've ever wondered what drives top racers who have dominated their sport for years, the answer is commitment. But be careful here. Consider a racer who has done everything in order to reach the number one slot at the end of the season: goal achieved, pinnacle reached. The next season they have the coveted '1' on their car or bike and expectations are high. But then the champion doesn't seem to be racing as well as they did last year, and is finishing fourth or sixth, or failing to finish at all. What has gone wrong? This may be as simple as not having a strategy or a set of process or performance goals for the current season. It is almost as if they're thinking, 'I have achieved my goal – now what?' My advice would be to focus on smaller elements of racing rather than the bigger picture in order to regain composure and return to winning ways.

What drives some racers to continue? (LAT)

Flow states: entering 'the zone'

If all the ingredients are in the same place at the same time, a racer will slip into 'the zone'. This is a place where everything seems to be effortless. You can turn sharper, brake later and get on the gas earlier than your competitors. You take the fastest line through the corners, hit the apex time after time, are poised and composed and almost in a trance-like state where time seems to slow down and decisions can be made easily. Everything that happens becomes second nature. These are signs that you are indeed in 'the zone', or in a state of flow, where performance is optimised and effortless.

In guiding racers through the concept of flow, I usually begin by asking them to think of a time during a race when everything seemed to gel or come together, where their performance oozed quality and they just knew that it was good. I then ask the racer to recall it from memory, with the help of the following statement:

'When I've been most content with my performance, I have felt at one with the car/bike, the track and everything. I was really tuned into what I was doing and

Is your racing seemingly effortless? You may be in 'the zone'. (sutton-images.com)

knew exactly how I was going to handle the race. I knew I had it all under control and I was completely aware of what everyone else was doing. I was totally absorbed in my driving/riding and I knew I was passing other drivers/riders but I didn't care – not that I didn't actually care, but rather I thought, "This is so cool" and I just drove/rode and won. I was in complete control of the situation. It felt really good.'

This is an example of a flow state. The mindset that accompanies flow aids in pushing a person to his or her limits. For the body to perform well, the mind must be focused.

The nine components of flow

According to Susan Jackson and Mihaly Csikszentmihalyi (1999), nine ingredients for optimal performance need to be in place for flow to occur. Let us look at each of these in turn specifically in relation to motorsport:

1 The challenge–skills balance

You should strike a balance between the challenge and your skills. It is not the reality of the challenges or skills that is important, but what you think of the opportunities and whether you have the capacity to act. So, if you think that the opportunity to pass is there but you do not have the skill to execute the pass at that moment in time or that place on the circuit, you should hang back. The challenge may be to remain consistent, or to gain experience specific to that circuit, or it may be to conserve tyres as the race progresses. Whatever the challenge, the need to be self-disciplined and to stay within limits is required.

2 Action-awareness merging

Your mind and body become one. There is no separation between what you are thinking and what your body is doing. You do not have to think about rhythmic breathing. Similarly, you should not have to think about how you are riding or driving, it should just be happening. Think about strategy rather than the process of riding or driving.

3 Setting clear goals

You should set clear goals in advance of the event. It is important that you know exactly what it is that you wish to achieve. Your goals should be specific and measurable. If goals are clear, you will be able to focus your attention on strategy, and consequently your concentration should remain for the duration of the session. Be aware that it may be necessary to set new goals for each session on the track. Visualising your performances in advance of the actual race is a useful way of focusing on clear goals. Examples include: staying near to the front; concentrating for the whole duration of the session; reacting quickly to attacks; knowing exactly which racers went in any breakaways; keeping at least three racers in view at all times (unless you are already lying first, second or third); and keeping the race under your control during critical times in the session. Chapter 8 is useful in setting such goals.

4 Unambiguous feedback

You should be aware of what is happening moment by moment. But remember, this may be an endurance event so you might not need to act on the information immediately. The human body will provide feedback if a racer tunes into its signals. Is your heart racing? If it is, take a few deep breaths. Is it still racing? Probably not. Can you feel arm pump? If yes, take some deep breaths to get oxygen to the muscles. Alternatively, try a dissociative strategy, *ie* focus on something other than the pain in your arms. Think of the racer in front and watch him, or assess your goals while on the move, and the pain miraculously disappears.

You may also obtain feedback from other racers. Use the information they provide to help you control your own race, but do *not* get sucked into their race. Remember that a racer might throw in some red herrings to put you off your pace, and of course, you might do the same.

5 Concentration on the task at hand

It goes without saying that concentration is critical to a task. You should think only of the task in hand, the current session etc. Avoid thinking too far ahead. Rather, think only of the moment. The aim is to become at one with the car or bike, inseparable. It becomes part of or an extension of you.

6 Sense of control

Ideally, you should have a sense of unlimited resources that will allow you to cope with anything that presents itself during the race. You should be able to control your performance and how you feel about it. You should have total composure. If you do not have unlimited resources, then you should use the resources you do have in a way that works for you. If you know you have stamina, for example, you should feel confident that this will shine through towards the end of each session, when other people may be getting tired or losing focus. A sense of control comes from your belief in your abilities. Avoid trying to gain control. Instead, focus on what you are capable of and let control emerge.

7 Loss of self-consciousness

If you are focusing on the task in hand, there will be no space left in your mind for self-consciousness ('How do I look?'), self-concern ('Am I doing this right?') or self-doubt ('Can I do this at all?'). When you gain a sense of control you will lose self-consciousness. This is a good thing! Avoid worrying about yourself, the car or bike, the team, or the crash fund. This will then free you up to engage fully in the race. You will be working on instinct. Evolution and survival of the fittest are based on instinct. Use it to your advantage.

8 Transformation of time

Dependence on time is a burden. We continually refer to our watches, and struggle to meet deadlines and appointments. This prevents us from engaging fully in our daily lives. When you get onto the track for your session, you should avoid mentally counting down the time (it is easy to get sucked into counting the number of laps as a way to knowing how long is left). To achieve flow, time should not matter (although lap times may be useful for goal setting). If you mentally count down the time left, it will drag (think of waiting

Just race! (David.WillowPhotography.co.uk)

for a kettle to boil). If you are in flow, time seems to speed up (so you get to the end of the session before you realise it). The following observation by an endurance-racer shows this: 'For each of my one-hour sessions in the eight-hour endurance race, I was in flow. It felt more like about five minutes. Time just seemed to pass me by.'

9 Autotelic experience ('I'm doing this for me')

When competitors are in a state of flow, they are not interested in rewards such as prize money, trophies or acclaim. The same should apply to you if you want to feel flow. Your reward is highly personal; you are doing this for yourself.

You pushed yourself and you beat yourself. There is no higher reward. Think of the Nike slogan and *just do it!* 'I got a real buzz.' 'That was great fun.' 'I feel like a champion.'

Now recall your own flow experiences

Write down your thoughts regarding the following (you are welcome to keep these private if you wish):

Think of a time when you were totally immersed in your driving or riding – a time when you felt strong and positive, not worried about crashing or failing. Describe the situation as fully as possible:

- When and where did it take place?
- Who were you with?
- What happened in the lead-up to the event?
- How did the experience start?

As you recall these experiences, use as many senses as possible to help you. Write down your thoughts, feelings and impressions of the experience, including how you felt afterwards.

An alternative, or perhaps complementary, way of exploring flow states is to use the questionnaire below. *The Flow State Scale (FSS)* is a measure of flow in sport and physical activity settings developed by in the 1990s (Jackson &

Csikszentmihalyi, 1999). The questions below are derived from this scale and aim to give you an idea of whether you had entered 'the zone' in any of your races. Don't worry if some of the questions appear to be asking the same thing.

Did my ability match the high challenge of the race?
Did I believe that my skills would allow me to meet the challenge?
Did I feel that I was competent enough to meet the high demands of the race?

You appear to have had the correct balance between challenge and skill

Did I race on 'autopilot' thinking automatically?
Did I employ the correct racing techniques without thinking about trying to do so?
Did I make moves spontaneously without having to think?

You appear to have been able to merge action with awareness

Did I know clearly what I wanted to do?
Were my goals clearly outlined?
Did I know exactly what I wanted to achieve during the race?

You appear to have had clear goals and were able to meet those goals

Was it clear that I was doing well during the race?
Did I know that I was achieving my objective?
Did I know how successfully I was racing?

You appear to have been able to obtain feedback on your performance

Was I able to keep my mind on what was happening effortlessly?
Did I have total concentration?
Was I completely focused on the job of racing?

You appear to have been able to concentrate and focus on your performance

Did I feel in total control of my racing?
Did I feel that I could control exactly what I was doing?
Did I feel in complete control of my car/bike?

You appear to have been able to exercise control over your performance

Was I concerned with what others may have been thinking of me?
Was I worried about my performance during the race?
Was I concerned with how I was presenting myself during the race?

You appear to have been able to overcome the feeling of 'self-consciousness'

Did it feel as if time didn't seem to matter?
Did it feel as if time had stopped while I was racing?
Did it seem as if things were happening in slow motion at times during the race?

You appear to have been able to over-ride the importance of time

Did the experience leave me feeling great?
Did I enjoy the feeling of that race and want to recapture it?
Did I find the experience extremely rewarding?

You appear to have been able to experience the feeling of 'just doing it'!

The more questions you have answered 'yes' to, the more likely it is that you were experiencing a 'flow state'. If you have answered 'no' to most of the questions, don't worry. At least you have more of an idea of the kind of elements that may help you to get into a 'flow state' during future races.

Closing comment

If you begin to think in this way, the rewards will just come as a consequence of your achieving flow states. Nothing else matters, only doing this for the right reasons.

There is a notion that racers should strive for perfection or that they are perfectionists. Perfection does not exist except in one's mind! Flow provides a glimpse of it. Flow is perhaps the closest to perfection that a racer is likely to attain. Imagine that perfection is represented by a narrow line or path that you will fall off if you don't get it right. Flow is more like operating within a window of opportunity. There are many ways through a situation, *not* a right way or a wrong way. Flow will allow you to perform within this window while other riders or drivers are becoming self-conscious because they are not balancing on their own narrow line.

As a sport psychologist, I would have to advise racers to avoid getting bogged down with the terminology outlined in the nine steps above. Rather, you should try to build the practical information into preparations for racing. If you try too hard you will not achieve flow!

And finally ...

The final statement I have to make is that although you have reached the end of this book, you have only reached the beginning of your journey of discovery. The performance profile from the previous chapter and the questionnaires provided elsewhere will act as a foundation for future progress. The guidance provided in each of the preceding chapters should feed into this performance profile.

Remain focused, remain positive and build on your existing skills, whether you are reading this as a novice or a highly experienced racer.

Seek flow rather than perfection. Flow is achievable, perfection is not! (LAT)

Bibliography

Anderson, A.G., Miles, A., Mahoney, C., and Robinson, P. (2002). 'Evaluating the Effectiveness of Applied Sport Psychology Practice: Making the Case for a Case Study Approach' *The Sport Psychologist* 16, pp.432–53.

Andersen, M.B. (ed) (2000). *Doing Sport Psychology*, Human Kinetics, Champaign.

Bandura, A. (1977). *Social-learning Theory*, Prentice-Hall, New Jersey.

Baumeister, R.F., and Tice, D.M. (1985). 'Self-esteem and Responses to Success and Failure: Subsequent Performance and Intrinsic Motivation' *Journal of Personality* 53 (3), pp.450–67.

Biddle, S.J.H. (ed) (1995). *European Perspectives on Exercise and Sport Psychology*, Human Kinetics, Champaign.

Biddle, S.J.H., and Mutrie, N. (2003). *Psychology of Physical Activity – Determinants, Well-being and Interventions*, Routledge, London.

Blumenstein, B., Bar-Eli, M., and Tenenbaum, G. (2002). *Brain and Body in Sport and Exercise: Biofeedback Applications in Performance Enhancement*, Wiley, New York.

Boyd, M.P., and Kim, M.-S. (2007). 'Goal Orientation and Sensation Seeking in relation to Optimal Mood States among Skateboarders' *Journal of Sport Behavior* 30 (1), pp.21–35.

Brewer, B.W., and Petitpas, A.J. (2005). 'Returning to Self: The Anxieties of Coming Back after Injury' in M.B. Andersen (ed), *Sport Psychology in Practice*, Human Kinetics, Champaign.

Buckworth, J., and Dishman, R.K. (2002). *Exercise Psychology*, Human Kinetics, Champaign.

Bull, S.J., Albinson, J.G., and Shambrook, C.J. (1996). *The Mental Game Plan: Getting Psyched for Sport*, Sports Dynamics, Eastbourne.

Butler, R.J., and Hardy, L. (1992). 'The Performance Profile: Theory and Application' *The Sport Psychologist* 6, pp.253–64.

Button, J. (2002). *Jenson Button: My Life on the Formula One Rollercoaster*, Bantam Press, London.

Carlson, N.R., Martin, G.N., and Buskitt, W. (2004). *Psychology* (2nd edition), Pearson, Harlow.

Carron, A.V., Bray, S.R., and Eys, M.A. (2002). 'Team Cohesion and Team Success in Sport' *Journal of Sports Sciences* 20, pp.119–26.

Cashmore, E. (2002). *Sport Psychology: The Key Concepts*, Routledge, London.

Clarke, N. (2000). *Nancy Clark's Sports Nutrition Guidebook*, Human Kinetics, Champaign.

Cockerill, I. (2002). *Solutions in Sport Psychology*, Thomson, London.

Conroy, D.E., and Coatsworth, J.D. (2007). 'Coaching Behaviours associated with Changes in Fear of Failure: Changes in Self-talk and Need Satisfaction as Potential Mechanisms' *Journal of Personality* 75 (2), pp.383–419.

Cox, R. (2007). *Sport Psychology: Concepts and Applications* (6th edition), McGraw Hill, Boston.

Cranwell-Ward, J., Bacon, A., and Mackie, R. (2002). *Inspiring Leadership*, Thomson, London.

Cumming, J., and Hall, C. (2002). 'Deliberate Imagery Practice: The Development of Imagery Skills in Competitive Athletes' *Journal of Sports Sciences* 20, pp.137–45.

Dale, G.A., and Wrisberg, C.A. (1996). 'The Use of a Performance Profiling Technique in a Team Setting: Getting Athletes and Coaches on the "Same Page"' *The Sport Psychologist* 10, pp.261–77.

Deci, E.L. (1976). *Intrinsic Motivation*, Plenum Press, New York.

Deppe, R.K., and Harackiewicz, J.M. (1996). 'Self-handicapping and Intrinsic Motivation: Buffering Intrinsic Motivation from the Threat of Failure' *Journal of Personality and Social Psychology* 70 (4), pp.868–76.

Duda, J.L., and Treasure, D.C. (2006). 'Toward Optimal Motivation in Sport: Fostering Athletes Competence and Sense of Control' in J.M. Williams (ed), *Applied Sport Psychology: Personal Growth to Peak Performance* (5th edition), Mayfield Publishing Company, Mountain View, California.

Easterbrook, J.A. (1959). 'The Effect of Emotion on Cue Utilisation and the Organisation of Behaviour' *Psychological Review* 66, pp.183–201.

Elliot, A.J., Cury, F., Fryer, J.W., and Huguet, P. (2006). 'Achievement Goals, Self-handicapping, and Performance Attainment: A Mediational Analysis' *Journal of Sport and Exercise Psychology* 28 (3), pp.344–61.

Ellis, A. (1962). *Reason and Emotion in Psychotherapy*, Lyle Stuart, New York.

Fletcher, D., and Hanton, S. (2003). 'Sources of Organisational Stress in Elite Performers' *The Sport Psychologist* 17, pp.175–95.

Francis, R.D. (2004). *Becoming a Psychologist*, Palgrave Macmillan, Basingstoke.

Gibson, J.J. (1979). *The Ecological Approach to Visual Perception*, Houghton Mifflin, Boston.

Gieremek, K., Osiadlo, G., Rudinska, A., and Nowotny, J. (1994). 'Physiological Responses to Selected Relaxation Techniques' *Biology of Sport* 11 (2), pp.109–13.

Gill, D. (2000). *Psychological Dynamics of Sport and Exercise*, Human Kinetics, Champaign.

Godden, D., and Baddeley, A.D. (1975). 'Context-dependent Memory in Two Natural Environments: On Land and Under Water' *British Journal of Psychology* 66, pp.325–31.

Gould, D.M. (2006). 'Goal Setting for Peak Performance' in J.M. Williams (ed), *Applied Sport Psychology: Personal Growth to Peak Performance* (5th edition), Mayfield Publishing Company, Mountain View, California.

Guillot, A., and Collet, C. (2005). 'Duration of Mentally Simulated Movement: A Review' *Journal of Motor Behaviour* 37 (1), pp.10–20.

Hagger, M., and Chatzisarantis, N. (2005). *The Social Psychology of Exercise and Sport*, Open University Press, London.

Hall, C., Mack, D., Paivio, A., and Hausenblas, H. (1998). 'Imagery Use by Athletes: Development of the Sports Imagery Questionnaire' *International Journal of Sport Psychology* 29, pp.73–89.

Hanin, Y.L. (2000). *Emotions in Sport*, Human Kinetics, Champaign.

Hardy, L., Jones, G., and Gould, D. (1996). *Understanding Psychological Preparation for Sport*, John Wiley and Sons, Chichester.

Holmes, P., and Collins, D. (2001). 'The PETTLEP Approach to Motor Imagery: A Functional Equivalence Model for Sport Psychologists' *Journal of Applied Sport Psychology* 13, pp.60–83.

Horn, T. (1992). *Advances in Sport Psychology*, Human Kinetics, Champaign.

Jackson, S.A., and Csikszentmihalyi, M. (1999). *Flow in Sports: The Keys to Optimal Experiences and Performances*, Human Kinetics, Champaign.

Jackson, S.A., and Marsh H.W. (1996). Development and validation of a scale to measure optimal experience: the flow state scale. *Journal of Sport and Exercise Psychology* 18 (1) pp. 17–35.

Jacobson, E. (1938). *Progressive Relaxation* (2nd edition), University of Chicago Press.

James, W. (1890). *Principles of Psychology* vol 1, Henry Holt, New York.

Jones, G., and Hardy, L. (1992). *Stress and Performance in Sport*, John Wiley and Sons, Chichester.

Jowdy, D.P., and Harris, D.V. (1990). 'Muscular Responses during Mental Imagery as a Function of Motor Skill Level' *Journal of Sport and Exercise Psychology* 12, pp.191–201.

Kerr, J.H. (1997). *Motivation and Emotion in Sport: Reversal Theory*, Psychology Press, Hove.

King, J.R. (1988). 'Anxiety Reduction Using Fragrances' in S. Van Toller and G. Dodd (eds), *Perfumery: The Psychology and Biology of Fragrance*, Chapman Hall, London.

Kohn, P. and Macdonald, J.E. (1992). The Survey of Life Experiences: A decontaminated hassles scale for adults. *Journal of Behavioral Medicine* 15, pp. 221–236.

Kohn, P.M., Lafreniere, K., and Gurevich, M. (1990). 'The Inventory of College Students' Recent Life Experiences: A Decontaminated Hassles Scale for a Special Population' *Journal of Behavioural Medicine* 13 (6), pp.619–30.

Kolb, B., and Whishaw, I.Q. (2003). *Fundamentals of Human Neuropsychology* (5th edition), Worth, New York.

Landers, D.M., and Arent, S. (2006). 'Arousal-Performance Relationships' in J.M. Williams (ed), *Applied Sport Psychology: Personal Growth to Peak Performance* (5th edition), Mayfield Publishing Company, Mountain View, California.

Lang, P.J., Kozak, M.J., Miller, G.A., Levin, D.N., and McLean, A. Jr. (1980). 'Emotional Imagery: Conceptual Structure and Pattern of Somato-Visceral Response' *Psychophysiology* 17 (2), pp.179–92.

Lavallee, D., Kremer, J., Moran, A.P., and Williams, M. (2004). *Sport Psychology: Contemporary Themes*, Palgrave Macmillan, New York.

Locke, E.A. (1991). 'Problems with Goal-Setting Research in Sports – and Their Solution' *Journal of sport and Exercise Psychology* 8, pp.311–16.

Locke, E.A., and Latham, G.P. (1985). 'The Application of Goal Setting to Sports' *Journal of Sport Psychology* 7, pp.205–22.

Loehr, J.E. (1995). *The New Mental Toughness Training For Sports*, Penguin, New York.

Mahoney, M.J., and Avener, M. (1977). 'Psychology of the Elite Athlete: An Exploratory Study' *Cognitive Therapy and Research* 1, pp.135–41.

Martens, R. (1987). *Coaches Guide to Sport Psychology*, Human Kinetics, Champaign.

Martens, R., Burton, D., Vealey, R.S., Bump, L.A., and Smith, D. (1990). 'Development and Validation of the Competitive State Anxiety Inventory–2' in R. Martens, R.S. Vealey, and D. Burton (eds), *Competitive Anxiety in Sport*, Human Kinetics, Champaign.

Maslow, A.H. (1970). *Motivation and Personality* (2nd edition), Harper and Row, New York.

Moran, A. (1996). *The Psychology of Concentration in Sports Performers: A Cognitive Analysis*, Psychology Press, Hove.

Morris, T., and Summers, J. (1995) *Sports Psychology: Theory, Applications and Issues*, John Wiley and Sons, Brisbane.

Murphy, S. (1995). *Sport Psychology Interventions*, Human Kinetics, Champaign.

Murphy, S. (2005). *The Sport Psych Handbook*, Human Kinetics, Champaign.

Nideffer, R.M. (1976). 'Test of Attentional and Interpersonal Style' *Journal of Personality and Social Psychology* 34, pp.394–404.

Nideffer, R.M., and Sagal, M.S. (2006). 'Concentration and Attention Control Training' in J.M. Williams (ed), *Applied Sport Psychology: Personal Growth to*

Peak Performance (5th edition), Mayfield Publishing Company, Mountain View, California.

Niven, A.G., and Owens, A. (2007). 'Qualification and Training Routes to becoming a Practising Sport and Exercise Psychologist in the UK' *Sport and Exercise Psychology Review* 3 (2), pp.47–50.

Orlick, T. (1990). *In Pursuit of Excellence*, Human Kinetics, Champaign.

Paivio, A. (1985). Cognitive and Motivational Functions of Imagery in Human Performance' *Canadian Journal of Applied Sport Sciences* 10, pp.225–85.

Pinel, J.P.J. (2003). *Biopsychology* (5th edition), Allyn and Bacon, New York.

Roberts, G.C. (2001). *Advances in Motivation in Sport and Exercise*, Human Kinetics, Champaign.

Sackett, R.S. (1934). 'The Influence of Symbolic Rehearsal upon the Retention of a Maze Habit' *Journal of General Psychology* 10, pp.376–95.

Schultz, J.H., and Luthe, W. (1959). *Autogenic Training: A Psychophysiological Approach to Psychotherapy*, Grune and Stratton, New York.

Selye, H. (1956). *The Stress of Life*, McGraw-Hill, New York.

Selye, H. (1983). 'The Stress Concept: Past, Present and Future' in C.L. Cooper (ed), *Stress Research*, Wiley, New York.

Sherman, C.P., and Poczwardowski, A. (2005). 'Integrating Mind and Body: Presenting Mental Skills to Young Teams' in M.B. Andersen (ed), *Sport Psychology in Practice*, Human Kinetics, Champaign.

Shin, D.S., and Lee, K.-H. (1994). 'A Comparative Study of Mental Toughness Between Elite and Non-Elite Female Athletes' *Korean Journal of Sport Science* 6, pp.85–102.

Singer, R.N., Hausenblas, H.A., and Janelle, C.M. (eds) (2001). *Handbook of Sport Psychology* (2nd edition), Wiley, New York.

Syer, J., and Connolly, C. (1986). *Sporting Body: Sporting Mind – An Athlete's Guide to Mental Training*, Simon and Schuster, New York.

Taylor, J., and Wilson, W. (eds) (2005). *Applying Sport Psychology: Four Perspectives*, Human Kinetics, Champaign.

Utay, J., and Miller, M. (2006). 'Guided Imagery as an Effective Therapeutic Technique: A Brief Review of its History and Efficacy Research' *Journal of Instructional Psychology* 33 (1), pp.40–3.

Vallerand, R.J., and Losier, G.F. (1999). 'An Integrative Analysis of Intrinsic and Extrinsic Motivation in Sport' *Journal of Applied Sport Psychology* 11, pp.142–69.

Vealey, R.S., and Greenleaf, C.A. (2006). 'Seeing is Believing: Understanding and using Imagery in Sport' in J.M. Williams (ed), *Applied Sport Psychology: Personal Growth to Peak Performance* (5th edition), Mayfield Publishing Company, Mountain View, California.

Weinberg, R.S., and Gould, D. (1999). *Foundations of Sport and Exercise Psychology* (2nd edition), Human Kinetics, Champaign.

Weinberg, R.S., and Gould, D. (2007). *Foundations of Sport and Exercise Psychology* (4th edition), Human Kinetics, Champaign.

Weinberg, R.S., and Williams, J.M. (2006). 'Integrating and Implementing a Psychological Skills Training Program' in J.M. Williams (ed), *Applied Sport Psychology: Personal Growth to Peak Performance* (5th edition), Mayfield Publishing Company, Mountain View, California.

West, J. (2005). 'Energising' mental imagery script, University of Worcester student handout (unpublished).

Whitaker, D. (1999). *The Spirit of Teams*, The Crowood Press, Ramsbury, Marlborough.

Williams, J.M., and Harris, D.V. (2006). Relaxation and Energizing Techniques for Regulation of Arousal' in J.M. Williams (ed), *Applied Sport Psychology: Personal Growth to Peak Performance* (5th edition), Mayfield Publishing Company, Mountain View, California.

Williams, J.M., and Straub, W.F. (2006). 'Sport Psychology: Past, Present, Future' in J.M. Williams (ed), *Applied Sport Psychology: Personal Growth to Peak Performance* (5th edition), Mayfield Publishing Company, Mountain View, California.

Zinsser, N., Bunker, L., and Williams, J.M. (2006). 'Cognitive Techniques for Building Confidence and Enhancing Performance' in J.M. Williams (ed), *Applied Sport Psychology: Personal Growth to Peak Performance* (5th edition), Mayfield Publishing Company, Mountain View, California.

Index